Windows of Wisdom

Devotional Studies in Proverbs

by Stephen F. Olford

This special edition is published by the Billy Graham Evangelistic Association with permission from the publisher, Ambassador-Emerald International.

AMBASSADOR-EMERALD INTERNATIONAL
GREENVILLE, SOUTH CAROLINA • BELFAST, NORTHERN IRELAND

Windows of Wisdom

Copyright © 2001 Stephen F. Olford

ISBN 1-59328-000-9
Previous ISBN: 1-889893-54-4

Published by:
Ambassador-Emerald International
427 Wade Hampton Blvd.
Greenville, SC 29609 USA

and

Ambassador Productions
Ardenlee Street
Belfast, Northern Ireland
BT6 8QJ

Cover and internal design by Brad Sherman
Cover design © 2001 Grand Design

Dedication

Windows of Wisdom
Is lovingly dedicated to

Heather Olford

A wonderful wife,
A precious partner,
A devoted mother,
A woman of God.

Contents

Preface

This devotional book, ***Windows of Wisdom***, was written during a titanic battle I had with cancer. Humanly speaking, the odds for remission, leave alone a cure, were dismally remote. During that whole period of powerful chemotherapy, my God sustained me by his Word and the Spirit day and night. When my soul melted from heaviness, my recurring prayer was *"Strengthen me according to Your word"* (Ps. 119:28).

There were many portions of scripture to which I was strangely drawn—and Proverbs was one of them. Perhaps the stated purpose of the book is the reason for this (1:3,5). It is to impart moral discernment and discretion and to develop mental clarity and perception (1:2,6). The two words "wisdom" and "instruction" complement each other. Wisdom means "skill," and instruction means "discipline." No skill is perfected without discipline. The most fundamental skill of all is *practical righteousness* in *every area of life*—including a bout with cancer.

What follows in these pages, therefore, is the "fleshing out" in expository form of the issues of life that are dealt with in this remarkable book. This "expository form," with homiletical structure, is purposely used to help Bible class leaders and pastors who are often pressed for material to teach or preach. So many devotional books today are anything but expositions of God's Word.

Alongside of the Word and the Spirit was a wonderful wife and precious partner *"comparable to [me]"* (Gen. 2:20). Heather suffered the entire "cancer ordeal" with me. For this one reason alone, this book is dedicated to her. For another, Heather has pleaded with me for years to write a devotional book!

One more matter. The concluding pages of this book give us a unique "window"—through which we observe the devotional life of Jesus in His perfect humanity. It reads: *"In the morning, having risen a long while before daylight, He went out and departed to a solitary place; and there He prayed"* (Mark 1:35). If Jesus, the God-Man, needed a place, a practice and a pattern for His devotional life, how much more you and me! So "Your Devotional Life" (pages 189-204) is a "must read" for you.

My prayer is that God will bless these **Windows of Wisdom** to all my readers for their good and God's glory.

Stephen F. Olford

Acknowledgments

My special thanks:

To my family and friends who have encouraged me to write **Windows of Wisdom**.

To the sources both cited and "forgotten" that have enabled me to weave the tapestry of each expository unit.

To Jennifer Balmer, my projects assistant, for her faithful and insightful commitment to typing and preparing the manuscript for publication.

To my publishers for their co-operation and creativity in making **Windows of Wisdom** a readable reality.

Finally, to my God—Father, Son, and Holy Spirit—Who has chosen to reveal Himself in the pages of Holy Scripture—to Whom be all the honor and glory forever.

Stephen F. Olford

Introduction

The book of Proverbs is a rich collection of biblical sayings on God's perspective for life. Each proverb is a window of wisdom shedding light on an eternal truth.

The key word in Proverbs is *wisdom*. It occurs, in English, some 54 times. "Wisdom" means "the ability to live life skillfully." Knowledge is one thing, but how to flesh out knowledge in everyday life requires divine wisdom.

As we walk through the corridors of this wonderful "palace" of Proverbs, with its windows of light and color on every side, some guidance is in order—if we would benefit spiritually from our *devotional* treatment of each chapter.

First, **read**. There are thirty–one chapters in Proverbs—one for each day of the month! Never tire of reading through this book of wisdom. Each devotional theme will be explained and applied from the selected verses that you are invited to read. Having these ready at hand will enable you to follow the expositions and meditations—and also look up helpful supporting references from the rest of Scripture.

Secondly, **look**. Each key word in the text of the day is a window of light on the meaning and message of God to our hearts. So look through each window to see the key word within its context, and then remember Proverbs 25:11, "A word fitly spoken is like apples of gold in pictures of silver" (KJV)!

Thirdly, *think*. Each devotional will be an exposition of the text and the application of the truth. In the busyness and bustle of life, we often fail to take time to "think" on spiritual things. Meditation seems to be a lost art! We must discipline ourselves to recapture this holy practice. With David the psalmist we must say, "Your testimonies are my meditation" (119:99).

Fourthly, *pray*. After thinking through what the Holy Spirit has said to us, we must pray for enabling grace to obey the truth that has been revealed to us. Let the testimony of our lives earn the commendation of the Christians at Rome concerning whom Paul the apostle could say, "The fame of *your obedience* has spread everywhere, and this makes me happy about you. I want you to be expert in goodness, but innocent in evil. . . . The grace of our Lord Jesus be with you" (Rom. 16:19-20, The Revised English Bible).

So I welcome you to **Windows of Wisdom**!

Stephen F. Olford

Knowledge

"The fear of the LORD is the beginning of knowledge, but fools despise wisdom and instruction"
Proverbs 1:7

Knowledge

"The fear of the LORD is the beginning of knowledge,
but fools despise wisdom and instruction"
Proverbs 1:7

Proverbs 1

We begin with today's text (1:7). It is about the *knowledge* of God. There is nothing more important in all of life than to know "the only true God, and Jesus Christ whom [He has] sent" (John 17:3). We learn two lessons from this verse:

The Beginning of Knowledge

"The fear of the LORD is the *beginning* of knowledge" (1:7). The word "beginning" is a Hebrew noun which denotes the first place in time, order, or rank. It stresses the importance of giving God *first* place in our lives. To *know* Him, we must *fear* Him. "The fear of the LORD" is a common expression in the Psalms and elsewhere and occurs fourteen times in this book of Proverbs. In this context, it means a *penitential* turning from sin. "The fear of the LORD is to *hate* evil" (8:13). The Bible calls this *repentance*. We can never know God and hang on to our sins at one and the same time. But to know God, we must also *trust* Him. This calls for a *reverential* trusting in God. "In the fear of the LORD there is strong *confidence*" or faith (14:26). So the knowledge of God begins with "repentance toward God and faith toward our Lord Jesus Christ" (Acts 20:21). Let us begin experiencing God today—by turning from our sins and trusting in our God. The complete fulfillment of our beings is knowing God. Indeed, Jesus said that this is *eternal life*. This life is endless, since knowing God requires an eternity to develop fully; and, more than this, the nature and quality of this life necessitate an eternal dimension. So whether it is here on earth, or later in heaven, the divine purpose for every Christian is *to know God*.

The Barrier to Knowledge

"Fools *despise* wisdom and instruction" (1:7). The second part of our text reveals the barrier to the knowledge of God. The word "fools" describes the unrepentant mindset that despises divine wisdom and instruction. You will recall that David tells us in two of his psalms that "the fool has said in his heart, 'There is no God'" (14:1; 53:1). The "fool" here is synonymous with a wicked person. He or she aggressively flouts personal independence from God and His commandments. Such an individual is the opposite of a *wise* man or woman. The attitude of a fool is illustrated in Genesis 25:34 where Esau *despised* his birthright and sold it for "one morsel of food." Even though afterwards he wanted to inherit the blessing, he was rejected, for "he found no place for repentance" (Heb. 12:16-17). The barrier to the knowledge of God is the unrepentant mind and the unbelieving heart. What a warning about barriers in our lives! Let us see to it that no sin-barrier ever robs us of knowing God through His dear Son Who died for us to break down all barriers, and rose again for us to bring us blessing.

O God, I really want to know You with all my mind, heart, and will. I repent of any sin barrier in my life and turn to You in simple faith in your Son Jesus Christ as Savior and Lord. I believe Your Word which declares that "this is eternal life . . . to know You, the only true God, and Jesus Christ whom You have sent." Amen.

Wisdom

"The Lord gives wisdom"
Proverbs 2:6

Wisdom

"The Lord gives wisdom"
Proverbs 2:6

Proverbs 2:1-9

L ife is quite meaningless without Divine wisdom. We need this wisdom to interpret life, death, and eternity. Worldly wisdom is "earthly, sensual, [and] demonic," whereas heavenly wisdom "is first pure, then peaceable, gentle, willing to yield, full of mercy and good fruits, without partiality and without hypocrisy" (James 3:15, 17).

God's Wisdom is a Gift to Be Possessed

"The Lord gives wisdom" (v. 6). To possess this wisdom we must fulfill certain conditions. Look at verses 1-4. We must *receive* God's wisdom (v. 1). This is where we fail so often. We "do not have because we do not ask" (James 4:2). We must *request* God's wisdom. We must "cry out" for discernment and "lift up [our] voice for understanding" (v. 3). God says, "You will seek Me and find Me, when you search for Me with all your heart" (Jer. 29:13). More than this, we must *research* God's wisdom. Like an eager miner, we must dig for "hidden treasures" in God's holy Word (v. 4). Each of these conditions is preceded with the participle "if"! Remember that God's spiritual blessings are always conditional.

God's Wisdom is a Goal to be Pursued

"The Lord gives wisdom" (v. 6) in order to *reveal* Himself to us. The conditions we have looked at are followed by the important word "then" (v. 5, 9). The first teaches us that wisdom reveals *the awesomeness of our God*—only with Divine wisdom do we understand "the fear of the Lord" (v. 5). In a day of irreverence and spiritual insensitivity, we need to contemplate the awesomeness of the God with Whom we have to do! Divine wisdom also reveals *the attributes of our God*. These are summed up in one statement: "the knowledge of God" (v. 5). Think *right now* of His nature and names; reflect upon His perfections and excellencies; worship Him in "the beauty of holiness" (Ps. 29:2). Divine wisdom likewise reveals *the activities of our God*. Among the many that could be enumerated in Scripture we are given several right here. God *speaks* wisdom to us

- "from His mouth come knowledge and understanding" (v. 6). "He stores up sound wisdom" in us (v. 7). Recall the times when you lack wisdom (James 1:5). He *sends* wisdom to us in times of danger and peril "to preserve the way of His saints" (v. 8). This brings us to our second "then" (v. 9). When we fulfill the conditions (mentioned above), God *reproduces* Himself *in* us with the sublime qualities of His "divine nature" (2 Pet. 1:4). Our text (v. 9) mentions three: "righteousness," "justice," and "equity." These three occur in the same order Proverbs 1:3 and suggest a course of action or way of life. The term "path" (v. 9) means "the way in which a chariot rolls." What a beautiful metaphor! Like a chariot rolling down the highway, we should display the characteristics of our God for all to see. In New Testament language, it is the outliving of the indwelling Christ. All this is possible because "in [Christ] are hidden all the treasures of *wisdom* and knowledge. . . . and [we] are complete in Him" (Col. 2:3, 9). There is no demand made upon our lives for which He is not adequate. Thanks be to God!

O God of "every good and perfect gift," I ask in faith for Your promised wisdom to meet my lack and my need today. May the chariot wheels of my life carry the moral qualities of "righteousness, justice, and equity" along "the highway" of Your perfect will. I pray—in Jesus' name. Amen.

Trust

"Trust in the Lord with all your heart, and lean not on your own understanding; in all your ways acknowledge Him, and He shall direct your paths"
Proverbs 3:5-6

Trust

"Trust in the Lord with all your heart, and lean not on your own understanding; in all your ways acknowledge Him, and He shall direct your paths"
Proverbs 3:5-6

Proverbs 3:1-6

No verses are better known and loved in the book of Proverbs than the two that invite our attention today. And there is a substantial reason for this. The subject is TRUST; and, therefore, "the fundamental principle of all religion." The New Testament reminds us that "without faith [trust] it is impossible to please [God], for he who comes to God must believe that He is, and that

He is a rewarder of those who diligently seek Him" (Heb. 11:6). With that in mind, the importance of our text presents a threefold challenge:

The Decision of Trust must be Foremost in Our Lives

"Trust in the Lord with all your heart, and lean not on your own understanding" (3:5). This is where you and I *must* begin. Trust must be *total*—"trust in the Lord with *all* your heart." The verb literally means "to cling to"; yes, with both arms! Along the Christian pathway, Jesus must have all of us. A handshake is not enough. But more than this, trust must be *focal*—"lean not on your own understanding" (v. 5). This is subtle, but immensely significant. The verb "lean" is used for a person who rests upon his spear for support and safety (2 Kings 7:2). As long as we can trust our spears or an officer who holds our spears, we are NOT trusting the Lord! No, trust must be total and focal.

The Devotion of Trust must be Fostered in our Lives

"In all your ways acknowledge Him" (3:6). By all the means of grace FAITH-TRUST must be fostered. We must live in the Scriptures (Rom. 10:17), we must look to the Savior (Heb. 12:2), and we must lean on the Spirit (Gal. 5:22). The proof that trust is growing is that we *acknowledge* the presence and pleasure of Christ in *all* our dealings and undertakings. The verb "acknowledge" literally means "to consciously know or recognize." This is no mere theoretical exercise. It is rather the total involvement of mind, heart, and will in holy synergism with the Savior. There must be no area in our lives where He cannot be welcomed and enjoyed. Paul sums it up perfectly when he exhorts, "Whether you eat or drink, or whatever you do, do all to the glory of God" (1 Cor. 10:31).

The Direction of Trust must be Followed in our Lives

"He shall direct your paths" (3:6). If our first two considerations are fleshed out in our lives, we can trust God to guide us in all our ways. The idea behind the word "direct" is that of making a way plain. In the Old Testament, it is used of God's power to remove obstructions (Isa. 49:11). The word is also employed to spell out the decree of a king. God not only removes obstructions, He also reveals instructions (Isa. 30:21; John 8:12). Needless to say, immediate *obedience* to all His instructions and commands demonstrates total and focal TRUST. You and I can know God-directed guidance every day of our lives! He created us "in Christ Jesus for good works . . . prepared beforehand that we should *walk* in them" (Eph. 2:10).

O Lord God, You created me to trust You. You directed me to trust You. Forgive me for allowing sin in my life to blur the vision of Your blessed Self as revealed in the face of Your Son. Focus my eyes on Jesus "the Author and Finisher of faith"—for His dear name's sake. Amen.

Discipline

*"My son give attention to
my words"*
Proverbs 4:20

Discipline

"My son give attention to my words"
Proverbs 4:20

Proverbs 4:20-27

The "father to son" sections appear frequently in the book of Proverbs. For this chapter, the dominating theme is that of *discipline*. Indeed, this is how the chapter begins: "Hear, my children, the instruction [literally "the *discipline*"] of a father" (v. 1). This is repeated in verse 10, and again in verses 20-24. If our lives are going to please our Father, then we must accept discipline over our hearts (v. 23), our lips (v. 24), our eyes (v. 25), and our feet (v. 26).

Our Hearts must be Guarded

"Keep your heart with all diligence" (v. 23). The heart is the center of our thinking (3:3; 6:21; 7:3), our feeling (15:15, 30), and our acting (11:20; 14:14), and so controls all of life. Out of the heart are "the issues of life" (v. 23). As our bodily health depends on the action of the heart, so our moral health depends on the function of the "new heart" (Ezek. 18:31). That is why we are to *guard* the heart "with *all* diligence" (v. 23). Only as we pray in the light of God's Word and live in the power of God's Spirit can the "peace of God . . . *guard* our hearts . . . through Christ Jesus" (Phil. 4:7). Paul's choice of this military term "guard" implies that the heart is the battle zone of our lives that must be protected by an "armed force."

Our Lips must be Governed

"Put away from you a deceitful mouth, and put perverse lips far from you" (v. 24). The mouth and lips are the vehicles through which the tongue functions. The apostle James reminds us that "if anyone does not stumble in *word*, he is a perfect man," but adds, "no man can tame the tongue" (James 3:2, 8). To govern the tongue is beyond human power. Only the ungrieved, unquenched Holy Spirit can guarantee mastery and self–control (Gal. 5:23). So we are commanded to "be filled [governed by] the Spirit" (Eph. 5:18).

Our Eyes must be Godly

"Let your eyes look straight ahead, and your eyelids look right before you" (v. 25). Jesus warned, "If your eye causes you to sin, pluck it out" (Matt. 18:9).

This is a call to drastic measures. To "look straight ahead" is a directive to practice simplicity of aim and singleness of motive. In New Testament language it is "looking unto Jesus" (Heb. 12:2). Only by focusing on Him can we develop "godly eyes." It was He who said: "The lamp of the body is the *eye*. Therefore, when your eye is good, your whole body also is full of light. . . . [and] having no part dark, the whole body will be full of light, as when the bright shining of a lamp gives you light" (Luke 11:34, 36). When we concentrate on what is *good* we are radiant (Ps. 34:5). We become like a light, the outshining of the One who declared, "I am the light of the world" (John 8:12). What do people see or sense when they look into our eyes?

Our Feet must be Guided

"Ponder the path of your feet. . . . Do not turn to the right or the left; remove your foot from evil" (vv. 26-27). To "ponder" means to "weigh conduct as in a balance." Before moving in any direction we must consider the nature and consequences of every step we take. We must be able to say with King David, "The steps of a good man are ordered by the Lord, and He delights in his way" (Ps. 37:23; Prov. 16:9). "Enoch walked with God" (Gen. 5:22) and "he had this testimony, that he *pleased* God" (Heb. 11:5).

O Lord, my God, You discipline me because you love me. Give me the grace to accept this discipline in every area of my life until I display "the peaceable fruit of righteousness" to the glory of Your name—through Jesus Christ my Lord. Amen.

Love

*"Drink waters from your own
cistern, and running water
from your own well"*
Proverbs 5:15

Love

"Drink waters from your own cistern, and running water from your own well"
Proverbs 5:15

Proverbs 5:15-18

Here is a chapter that deals daringly and delicately with the theme of married love. In language which is poetic, romantic, and symbolic, God reveals His divine purpose in love and marriage. The message becomes clear and challenging as we examine what "the Holy Spirit teaches, comparing spiritual things with spiritual" (1 Cor. 2:13).

Divine Love Condemns Lustful Marriage

"Drink waters from your *own* cistern" (v. 15). The key word here is the pronoun "own"—interpreting the first half of the chapter (vv. 1-14). The apostle Paul states the same truth when he writes about a leader being "the husband of one wife" (1 Tim. 3:2)—literally a "one-woman man." Indeed he goes on to assert that outside of God's purpose for marriage, "it is good for a man *not to touch* a woman" (1 Cor. 7:1). The verb "to touch" means "to set on fire"—which is nothing less than lustful marriage. You ask why, and the apostle answers: "Do you not know that your bodies are members of Christ? Shall I then take the members of Christ and make them members of a harlot? Certainly not! Or do you not know that he who is joined to a harlot is *one body with her*? For 'the two,' He says, 'shall become one flesh'" (1 Cor. 6:15-16). Little wonder that in our reading lustful marriage is described as: *seductive*—"For the lips of an immoral woman drip honey" (v. 3);—"but in the end she is bitter as wormwood" (v. 4); *sinful*—"Her feet go down to death" (v. 5), and we know that "the wages of sin is death" (Rom. 6:23) and "her steps lay hold of hell" (v. 5); *senseless*—"Her ways are unstable; you do not know them" (v. 6)—her steps willfully and senselessly stagger on her way to destruction (see also vv. 7-14); *shameful*—"streams of water in the streets" (v. 16). This last figure of speech says it all. It refers to the inevitable consequences of lustful marriage: illegitimate street children of harlotry! Well does God say, "Marriage is honorable among all, and the bed undefiled; *but fornicators and adulterers God will judge*" (Heb. 13:4).

Divine Love Commends Lawful Marriage

"Drink waters from your own cistern, and running water out of your own *well*" (v. 15). In both oriental and scriptural usage the wife is compared with a "cistern" and a "well" (Song of Sol. 4:12; 1 Pet. 3:7). And, in contrast to the lustful marriage, the "one-woman man" is exhorted to enjoy his wife with *the satisfying purity of love*—"running water out of your *own* well" (v. 15); *the satisfying dignity of love*—"let them [your children] be *only* your own" (v. 17); *the satisfying liberty of love*—"let your fountain be blessed" (v. 18); *the satisfying unity of love*— "rejoice *with* the wife of your youth" (v. 18); and *the satisfying constancy of love*—"*always* be enraptured with her love" (v. 19). What a picture, what a purpose, and what a pleasure in the quality of married love that our great God has intended! Where the laws of the universe are rejected there is tragedy; where they are respected there is victory!

In a day of lowered standards, shattered marriages, and broken homes, we need to return to the lofty scriptural principles we have considered in today's meditation. Only then shall we "drink water from [our] own cistern, and running water from [our] own well. . . . and rejoice with the wife of [our] youth" (vv. 15,18). Let it be stressed, once more, that these scriptural principles are not *human* suggestions, but *holy* instructions! The blessing of God on your marriage, family and future depend upon your *obedience* to God's Word.

O God of love, shed abroad in my heart, by Your indwelling Spirit, Your pure, warm, and strong love that I may love even as Christ loved the church and gave | *31*

Himself up for her. May such love be so irresistibly reciprocated that everyone in my family will love one another as You have loved me. I pray this in Jesus' name and for His sake alone. Amen.

Hate

"These six things the Lord hates, yes, seven are an abomination to Him"
Proverbs 6:16

Hate

"These six things the Lord hates, yes, seven are an abomination to Him"
Proverbs 6:16

Proverbs 6:12-19

A t first sight the words of our text startle us! It seems inconceivable, if not inconsistent, for God to hate! Yet as we examine the context and the rest of Scripture we see that there is "a time to hate" (Eccl. 3:8), and that the Bible is justified in teaching us to "hate the evil, [and] love the good" (Amos 5:15).

There are Things that We must Hate

"These . . . *things* the Lord hates" (v. 16). God alone has the sovereign prerogative to think, feel and act according to His own pleasure and purpose. As humans, we can only exclaim, "Oh, the depth of the riches both of the wisdom and knowledge of God! How unsearchable are His judgments and His ways past finding out! 'For who has known the mind of the Lord? Or who has become His counselor?'" (Rom. 11:33-34). With this lofty concept of our God we can readily see that God alone has the right to *describe* the hateful. The "worthless" and "wicked" man portrayed in verses 12-14 has prostituted his potential for good beyond the point of no return. He has employed speech, signs, and subtleties to devise mischief and sow discord. Having personified what is hateful, God now *defines* the seven things that are hateful to Himself and to all those who fear the Lord (vv. 16-17). Seven is the number of completeness and so intensifies the holy hatred of Almighty God against the things that are named. 1) There is *vanity*—"a proud look" (v. 17); 2) There is *falsity*—"a lying tongue" (v. 17); 3) There is *cruelty*—"hands that shed innocent blood" (v. 17); 4) There is *subtlety*—"a heart that devises wicked plans" (v. 18); 5) There is *villainy*—"feet that are swift . . . to evil" (v. 18); 6) There is *perjury*—"a false witness" (v. 19); 7) There is *enmity*—"one who sows discord among brethren" (v. 19). This last one God calls "an abomination." This word is the Bible's strongest expression of hatred (see Rev. 21:27). We need to think of this when we cause division in the family, the church, or the community! Contrast the blessing of God upon those who live together in peace (Ps. 133). Finally, God *alone* has the right to *destroy* what is hateful (v. 15). What God describes as hateful and what God destroys as hateful give us the clue to what we *must* hate.

There are Times when We must Hate

"The Lord hates" (6:16). In the final analysis, we cannot define God. The Infinite cannot be reduced to the finite. What we do know, however, is that "God is Spirit [or 'Life']" (John 4:24); "God is Light" (1 John 1:5); and "God is Love" (1 John 4:8). This means that *when* God hates, He does so with due regard to His nature as Life, Light, and Love. When He expresses His nature as Life, He hates sin with absolute *dignity*—because "He is King of kings . . . who alone has *immortality*" (1 Tim. 6:15-16). When He expresses His nature as Light, He hates sin with absolute *purity*—because He dwells "in unapproachable *light*" (1 Tim. 6:16). When He expresses His nature as Love, He hates sin with absolute *jealousy*—because the Lord God is "a *jealous* God, visiting the iniquity . . . of those who *hate* [Him], but showing mercy . . . to those who love [Him]" (Exod. 20:5-6). Divine jealousy is love's burning zeal to "do *all* to the glory of God" (1 Cor. 10:31). If you and I are to be identified with the Lord of Life, Light, and Love, we also will have to "hate evil, [and] love good" (Amos 5:15). Under His lordship, we must live out the abhorrence of sin by the power of the Holy Spirit Who alone can set us "free from the law of sin and death" (Rom. 8:2). Remember, there are *things* to hate and *times* to hate.

King of kings and Lord of lords, my heart has been convicted and chastened by the truth of Your Word. I have seen afresh how You hate sin, while You still love the sinner. Create in me a holy abhorrence of evil that I may love what You love and hate what You hate. I pray this in the name of Jesus. Amen.

Obedience

"My son, keep my words, and treasure my commands within you"
Proverbs 7:1

Obedience

"My son, keep my words, and treasure my commands within you"
Proverbs 7:1

Proverbs 7:1-5

Obedience is love's *active* response to *all* the will of God—with joyful anticipation (John 14:15). That is our theme in this chapter in a context of a sex–satiated, sordid, and sinful world (see verses 6-23). For young and old alike, obedience to God's "words," "commands," and "laws" is the only hope for a life of purity and victory.

The Demands of Obedience

"My son, keep my words, and treasure my commands within you. Keep my commands and live, and my law as the apple of your eye. Bind them on your fingers; write them on the table of your heart" (vv. 1-3). Our all-wise and loving Father addresses us as sons and daughters and clearly lays down the demands of true obedience. First, we must *receive* the Word of God. We must "keep" and "treasure" God's "words" and "commands" (vv. 1-2). Secondly, we must *reflect* the Word of God—"Keep . . . my law as the apple of your eye" (v. 2). This proverbial figure of speech, "the apple of your eye," is the miniature reflection of objects seen in the pupils of another's eye. As we look into God's Word day by day, people should be able to see reflected and protected what the Holy Spirit is effecting in our lives (see 2 Cor. 3:18). Thirdly, we must *relate* the Word of God—"Bind them on your fingers; write them on the table of your heart" (v. 3). This refers to the little leather containers secured to the middle finger and forehead of godly Jews to remind them in their times of prayer and meditation that their *outward life*, "the fingers," and *inward life*, "the heart," should be under the authority of God's law. In those little leather containers were strips of parchment on which were inscribed portions of the Torah (five books of Moses).

The Delights of Obedience

"Keep my commands and *live*" (v. 2). "Trust and obey, for there's no other way to be happy in Jesus, but to trust and obey." The delights of obedience are summed up in two words: *vitality* and *longevity* of life. In Old Testament times, God honored His people's obedience with material and physical benefits as well as spiritual blessings. For us today, obedience is rewarded with the *blessings* of the Spirit—initially (Eph 1:3) and continually (Eph. 5:18). This is *vitality* in the Christian life! Obedience is also rewarded with the *benefits* of the Spirit (Rom. 8:11; Phil. 3:10) "Being spiritually–minded means overcoming the deadness of the body and experiencing life and peace. This is the resurrection life" for *now* and hereafter (The Nelson Study Bible, p. 1892). It matters little how long we live—as long as we *live well*. This is *longevity* in the Christian life!

The Dynamics of Obedience

"Say to wisdom, 'You are my sister,' and call understanding your nearest kin, that they may keep you from the immoral woman, from the seductress who flatters with her words" (7:4-5). These verses suggest the two motivations that undergird obedience to the Word of God and, therefore, a life of purity (v. 5). The first is *the word of encouragement*—"Say to wisdom, 'You are my sister'" (v. 4). Wisdom is here personified as "my sister." Jesus called those who do the will of God His "brother," "*sister*," and "mother" (Matt. 12:50). We all know the singular role that a sister plays in the circle of the family; it is that *wise* word of encouragement! Then there is *the wound of admonishment*—"Call understanding your nearest kin" (v. 4). The Hebrew means "familiar friend." And in this book of Proverbs we are reminded that "faithful are the wounds of a friend" (27:6). It is from a "*faithful* friend" that we best receive the wound of admonishment. Here, then, are the dynamics of obedience. Sacrifice, however good or great, can never take the place of an *obedient* life (see 1 Sam. 15:22).

Lord Jesus, in Your humanity You "learned obedience by the things that You suffered—even to the death of the cross." Teach me; yes, train me to obey Your holy Word and will—whenever the call, or whatever the cost, for Your dear name's sake. Amen.

Happiness

*"Now therefore, listen to me,
my children, for blessed are
those who keep my ways"*
Proverbs 8:32

Happiness

*"Now therefore, listen to me, my children, for blessed
are those who keep my ways"*
Proverbs 8:32

Proverbs 8:32-36

There is a difference between joy and happiness. Joy is a spiritual quality, and, therefore, the constant state of a Spirit-filled life. Happiness is the emotional expression of that state and is sometimes affected by the pleasures and problems of daily happenings. But Jesus clearly taught in His Beatitudes (Matt. 5:3-12) that heaven's happiness is for here and now.

The Imperatives of Happiness

"Now therefore, listen to me, my children, for blessed are those who keep my ways. Hear instruction and be wise, and do not disdain it. Blessed is the man who listens to me, watching daily at my gates, waiting at the posts of my doors. For whoever finds me finds life, and obtains favor from the Lord" (8:32-35). Solomon concludes this chapter with an exquisite eulogy to the supremacy, activity, and eternity of divine *wisdom* (see verses 1-31). Throughout his phrasing, he personalizes this attribute to identify with what we know of our Lord Jesus Christ as the Source of all happiness or blessedness. He then outlines in didactic language the imperatives that lead to this happiness. First there must be *a spiritual relationship*—"Listen to me, *my children*" (v. 32). Until that relationship is established, the ways of wisdom can never be understood. It was to a religious scholar that Jesus said, "Unless one is born again, he cannot see the kingdom of God" (John 3:3). Secondly, there must be *a personal discipleship*—"Hear instruction and be wise, and do not disdain it" (v. 33). Personal discipleship involves *the happiness of learning*—"Blessed [happy] is the man who listens to me" (v. 34). Nothing will substitute for the discipline of learning. Personal discipleship involves *the happiness of loving*—"watching daily at my gates, waiting at the posts of my doors" (v. 34). These two descriptive sentences have been variously interpreted, but the obvious picture they convey is that of a lover watching and waiting for her beloved. This is how happiness grows (see Song of Sol. 3:1-4). Personal discipleship involves *the happiness of living*, "for whoever finds me finds life, and obtains the favor of the Lord" (v. 35). Here is the ultimate reason for attending on instruction from the Source of all wisdom—even our Lord Jesus Christ. In His high priestly prayer Jesus affirmed that "this is eternal life, that they may know You, the only true God, and Jesus Christ whom You have sent" (John 17:3). This, then, is the happiness of living!

The Alternatives to Happiness

"He who sins against me wrongs his own soul; all those who hate me love death" (v. 36). Because of the depravity of the human heart, people imagine that they can find happiness on their own terms; but God's faithful Spirit warns of the solemn alternatives to happiness. There is *the evil of self-deceitfulness*—"He who sins against me wrongs his own soul" (v. 36). We deceive ourselves when we think that we can sin against the Lord with impunity. It is true that we grieve the heart of God, but what we fail to realize is that we also injure our own souls. The longer we maintain this attitude of rebellion, the more insensitive we become to the pleadings of the Spirit. This leads to *the peril of self-destructiveness*—"All those who hate me love death" (v. 36). Those who will not listen to the voice of wisdom implicitly love death because they love the very things which lead to death. "He who believes in the Son has everlasting life; and *he who does not believe the Son shall not see life*, but the wrath of God abides on him" (John 3:36). These are stern words, but they come from the lips of incarnate Love. The person who refuses to believe on the Son of God and fails to "keep [His] ways" of true happiness, is headed for moral suicide. The alternative is simple and sure: "Happy is he who keeps the law" (Prov. 29:18b).

O God, You inhabit the eternal realms of happiness. "In Your presence is fullness of joy; at Your right hand are pleasures forevermore." I bless You that in Your purpose of grace You desire to share Your happiness with me here on earth, and then forevermore in glory. I thank You that "happy is he who keeps Your law." Amen.

Holiness

"The fear of the Lord is the beginning of wisdom: and the knowledge of the Holy One is understanding"
Proverbs 9:10

Holiness

*"The fear of the Lord is the beginning of wisdom: and
the knowledge of the Holy One is understanding"*
Proverbs 9:10

Proverbs 9:1-12

This is a climactic chapter in parabolic form that contrasts wisdom and
folly (i.e., verses 1-12 and 13-18). At the center of these two sections is our
devotional verse for today. The subject is holiness (v. 10). The term "Holy
One" is an intensive plural of the word for "holy"; literally "the Most Holy
One," or "the quintessence of holiness." And for those of us who know our

Bibles, we hear God saying, "It is written, be holy; for I am holy" (Lev. 11:44; 1 Pet. 1:16). What does this mean for you and me?

We must Sense the Holy One

"The fear of the Lord is the beginning of wisdom and the knowledge of the Holy One" (v. 10). As we approach this subject of holiness we must come with *a sense of reverence* for "God is greatly to be feared in the assembly of saints, and to be held in *reverence* by all those who are around Him" (Ps. 89:7). Reverence means "holy respect." The same idea is conveyed in the New Testament where we are exhorted to "serve God acceptably with *reverence* and godly fear" (Heb. 12:28). Our God is a holy God, and we should have a moral repugnance to any dishonorable act (Prov. 8:13). With this sense of reverence, we must also approach the standard of holiness with *a sense of confidence* – "In the fear of the Lord, there is strong confidence" (Prov. 14:26). If we are walking under an unclouded heaven, with the ungrieved, unquenched Holy Spirit filling our lives, we can "come boldly to the throne of grace [to] obtain mercy and find grace in time of need" (Heb. 4:16).

We must Seek the Holy One

"The knowledge of the Holy One" (v. 10). To know holiness, we must seek the Holy One. So often we think of holiness as a quality or an attribute; but holiness is more than that. Holiness is a *person* – "The Holy One." God, in Christ Jesus, has become our "sanctification" [holiness] (1 Cor. 1:30). As He, and He alone, lives in us by the Holy Spirit, we manifest in our behavior patterns the characteristics of holiness. So there must be "the *knowledge* of the Holy One" (v. 10). This calls for *intimate knowledge* – "The Lord loves you, ... therefore *know* that the Lord your God, He is God, the faithful God" (Deut. 7:8-9). That verb occurs 944 times in the Old Testament and is employed, among other ways, to describe the intimate union between husband and wife. This, in turn, leads to *consummate knowledge* – "I *know*," cried Job, "that my Redeemer [Vindicator] lives, and He shall stand at last on the earth" (Job 19:26). That is consummate knowledge! If we would be holy, we must seek the Holy One.

We must Serve the Holy One

"The knowledge of the Holy One is *understanding*" (v. 10). Understanding means "to separate mentally or to distinguish." When we really know the Holy One, we choose Whom we will serve! And we do so with *holiness* of life in our *walk*, "Be holy in all your conduct" (1 Pet. 1:15); our *worship*—"Pray everywhere, lifting up holy hands" (1 Tim 2:8); our *work*—"We commend ourselves as ministers of God .... by purity" (2 Cor. 6:4, 6); our witness—"You shall receive power when the Holy Spirit has come upon you; and you shall be witnesses" (Acts 1:8). What a call to holiness!

O most holy and awesome God, like the prophet Isaiah I have seen the Lord sitting on the throne high and lifted up, and I have heard the seraphim cry: "Holy, holy, holy is the Lord of hosts." Cleanse me from my unworthiness with the live coal from off Your altar, and use me to go and tell people of Your grace and glory. I pray in Jesus' name. Amen.

Diligence

*"He who has a slack hand
becomes poor, but the hand of
the diligent makes rich"*
Proverbs 10:4

Diligence

*"He who has a slack hand becomes poor, but the hand
of the diligent makes rich"*
Proverbs 10:4

Proverbs 10:1-6

Our "focus word" for today is the quality of *diligence*. Five times it occurs in the book of Proverbs and always means "the sharp pointed and determined activity of a truly dedicated person." As we examine these five mentions, each facet of this jewel reflects an aspect of truth which helps us to understand the word in its biblical and practical significance.

The Life of Practical Industry

"He who has a slack hand becomes poor, but the hand of the diligent makes rich." (10:4). By the use of contrast, Solomon teaches that industry clearly distinguishes between the lazy hand of indolence and the *busy* hand of diligence. In passage after passage the lazy man is searchingly exposed and soundly condemned, while the industrious man is rewarded and commended.

The Life of Personal Mastery

"The hand of the diligent will *rule*, but the lazy man will be put to forced labor" (12:24). The Holy Spirit here warns that slothfulness leads to slavery, whereas diligence guarantees mastery. Only the person who has *identified* Himself with Christ in His vicarious death and victorious resurrection can "reign in life" and, therefore, rule by the power of that same living Lord (Rom. 5:17b).

The Life of Powerful Victory

"The lazy man does not roast what he took in hunting, but diligence is man's precious possession" (12:27). The slothful man traps his prey but loses his roast, while the diligent man always enjoys the fruit of his victory. It is the privilege of the believer to follow in the "train" of the Savior's triumph in every situation (see 2 Cor. 2:14). This is the life of powerful victory (see Prov. 15:19; 18:9-11; 19:15-24).

The Life of Passional Quality

"The soul of a lazy man desires, and has nothing; but the *soul* of the diligent shall be made rich" (13:4). Nothing is more demoralizing than empty dreams and shattered hopes, but this is the inevitable portion of the sluggard. On the other hand, the soul of the diligent is made rich. When a person applies the qualities of diligence to all his living and serving, there will be both soul satisfaction and dedication. Divine passion is the explosive power of a holy dedication to make all this happen!

The Life of Purposeful Constancy

"The plans of the diligent lead surely to plenty, but those of everyone who is hasty, surely to poverty" (21:5). The words "plans" and "hasty" are incompatible. The diligent man weighs all the issues and then makes his decision. On the other hand, the thoughtless person acts hastily and has nothing to show. Purposeful constancy demands the diligence that leads to the abounding and abiding blessing of the Lord.

Diligence is a call to a life of practical industry, personal mastery, powerful victory, passional quality and, most important of all, purposeful constancy. God enable us, by the power of His indwelling Spirit, to "be diligent to be found by Him in peace, without spot and blameless" (2 Pet. 3:14).

Heavenly Father, with mind, heart, and will I respond to Your call for diligence in my life. I appeal to You as the Giver of every perfect gift, to develop in me the quality of diligence that will make me strive for excellence in all I say and do day by day. I pray in the strong name of Your Son. Amen.

Soul-Winning

"The fruit of the righteous is a tree of life, and he who wins souls is wise"
Proverbs 11:30

Soul-Winning

"The fruit of the righteous is a tree of life, and he who wins souls is wise"
Proverbs 11:30

Proverbs 11:27-31

This is the soul-winner's best known text in the Old Testament. If we view the Bible as a whole, we see that the Old Testament is the New Testament concealed, and the New Testament is the Old Testament revealed. Evangelical truth in the New Testament has its root in the Old. In our verse for today, we have three aspects of soul-winning that are suggested by New Testament teaching.

The Influence of Soul-Winning

"The fruit of the righteous is a tree of life" (v. 30). "The tree of life" symbolizes the influence of a godly life. Only when a person becomes righteous, through faith in the Lord Jesus Christ and abides in Him (John 15:4), can he reproduce the fruit of the tree of life. This fruit is *Jesus* made visible in us and through us by the power of the Holy Spirit. Only as we draw from the resources of a Spirit-filled life can we exude the irresistible influence of freshness, fragrance, and fruitfulness that will *draw* people to Christ (see John 12:32).

The Competence of Soul-Winning

"And he who wins souls is wise" (v. 30). This can also read, "He that is wise wins souls." Wisdom is the right use of knowledge, so knowledge without wisdom can be dangerous. The secret of wisdom is not only studying, but *mastering* the Word of God in personal experience. The competence of the soul-winner is not only that of knowing what to do, but actually doing the job. Knowledge is one thing, experience another. In the verb "to win" we have a clue to this "experience." The word has a military ring about it. It is used for capturing people for *evil* purposes (see 2 Tim. 2:26). But here, in our text, it has a positive connotation. It carries the idea of "rescue operations" – "to take alive" as in Luke 5:10. When Jesus plotted "rescue operations" to save souls from the devil's grasp and grip, He issued instructions like this: "No one can enter a strong man's house and plunder his goods, unless he first binds the strong man. And then he will plunder his house" (Mark 3:27). First, we must *enter the house*. This is a call to arms; it is aggressive evangelism. Second, we must *engage the hostility*—

"[Bind] the strong man." Only Jesus can do this, and, indeed, He has done it! "For this purpose the Son of God was manifested, that He might destroy the works of the devil" (1 John 3:8). The word "destroy" means "to loose," "dissolve," "sever," "break," "demolish"! Let us then claim these glorious words, "He who is in [us] is greater than he who is in the world" (1 John 4:4). Third, we must *emancipate the hostages*—"plunder his goods." That is our task as soul-winners. We are to "snatch" hostages from the enemy's grasp and minister to them, that they in turn and in time will be wise to win souls!

The Recompense of Soul-Winning

"The righteous will be recompensed on the earth" (v. 31). A soul-winner recognizes that there is recompense for a job well done. Quite apart from the *sense* of reward that we have here upon earth, there is going to be a time of recompense when we stand before the judgment seat of Christ. Those who have been faithful will receive the commendation of the Master as well as the conferred capacity to shine forever (see Dan. 12:3). As a soul-winner, the great apostle Paul could look forward to that day with joyful expectation—"What is our hope, or joy, or crown of rejoicing? Is it not even you in the presence of our Lord Jesus Christ at His coming?" (1 Thess. 2:19). Can you look on to that rewarding day and exclaim, "You are our glory and joy" (1 Thess. 2:20)?

Lord, Jesus, You came into the world to "seek and to save that which was lost." Endue me with that same soul-winning Spirit. May I endeavor to be "wise" to "become all things to all men that I may by all means save some." I pray this for Your glory. Amen.

Encourage-ment

"*Anxiety in the heart of man causes depression, but a good word makes it glad*"
Proverbs 12:25

Encouragement

"Anxiety in the heart of man causes depression, but a good word makes it glad"
Proverbs 12:25

Proverbs 12:18-25

We have touched on this theme of encouragement before; but today's text brings it back to our attention for further examination and instruction. A "good word" of encouragement is like "cold water to a weary soul, [and] good news from a far country" (Prov. 25:25).

The Weight of Discouragement

"Anxiety in the heart of man causes *depression*" (v. 25). "Anxiety" ("heaviness" KJV), when allowed to weigh upon us affects spirit, soul, and body. It is used in the Old Testament to describe "the feeling of melting away in terror." For example, the inconsolable worry of a parent looking for a lost son (1 Sam. 9:5; 10:21) and Zedekiah's terrifying fear of being considered a traitor (Jer. 38:19). This is the ultimate in discouragement. Discouragement *oppresses the spirit*. When Eliphas accused Job of folly, it turned his "spirit against God" (Job 15:13). This is one of the devil's devices to oppress us. Discouragement *depresses the soul*. When Job was overwhelmed with the misery heaped upon him he longed for death "to the bitter[ness] of soul" (Job 3:20). Discouragement *distresses the body*. When King David suffered under the divine hand of chastening, he had to admit, "There is no soundness in my flesh ... nor any health in my bones" (Ps. 38:3). This is what Solomon is talking about when he says, "Anxiety in the heart of man causes depression" (v. 25).

The Word of Encouragement

"A *good word* makes it glad" (v. 25). Few Christian gifts in the church inspire hope, joy, and peace like this jewel of encouragement. When Solomon chose his language for our text, he selected the most general of words in the entire Hebrew Old Testament! It occurs more than 1,400 times and is translated by no less than 85 different shades of meaning in our various versions. The ten commandments are actually "ten words"! Perhaps the significance of all this is to show how many words can be used to encourage people! Be that as it may, the "good word" of encouragement is God's precious gift to His church. One of the great encouragers of the New Testament was a man called Joses, who was also called Barnabas by the apostles, which translated is "son of encouragement" (see Acts 9:26-27; 11:22-24, 30 and chapters 13-15). The word "encouragement" in the New Testament reveals three aspects of this "good word." There is the *good word of counsel* (Acts 18:27). The Ephesian Christians wrote to *counsel* their Corinthian brethren concerning Apollos, that he was to be received and helped. Such counsel is always an encouragement. There is the *good word of courage* (1 Thess. 2:11-12). Writing to his young converts Paul could say, "We exhorted, and comforted, and charged every one of you. . . . that you would . . . walk worthy of God." How often such a "good word" has made the difference between failure and victory in our lives! There is the *good word of comfort* (John 11:19, 31). At the grave of Lazarus, "many of the Jews had joined . . . Martha and Mary, to comfort them concerning their brother." This consoling ministry is for those of us who are called to "rejoice with those who rejoice, and weep with those who weep" (Rom. 12:15).

The night my father died, I was conducting an evangelistic crusade in the city of Norwich in England. One evening before I stepped up to preach, my mother phoned through from Cardiff, Wales to say, "Your Father, in his last breath, asked me to give you this message: 'Tell the lad to "preach the Word"!' "

The next hour I was doing just that! That "good word" transformed my entire ministry forever!

O Lord Jesus Christ, You always had "a good word" for the saddened heart, broken spirit, and fearful soul. Teach me that "good word" in season and out of season—that I may be an encourager of others—for Your name's sake. Amen.

Pretense

"There is one who makes himself rich, yet has nothing; and one who makes himself poor, yet has great riches"
Proverbs 13:7

Pretense

"There is one who makes himself rich, yet has nothing; and one who makes himself poor, yet has great riches"
Proverbs 13:7

Proverbs 13:1-7

In today's text we have two contrasting weaknesses that each of us will find in the heart—if we are truly honest! In a word, it is the sin of *pretense*. It is the unreal image we project so often to others concerning our personas, positions, or possessions without factual substantiation. Here we have two aspects of pretense.

The Conceit of Pretense

"There is one who *makes* himself rich, yet has nothing" (v. 7). The root verb "to make" means, "to feign" or "pretend." This trait is part of our Adamic nature. Some mask it more than others; but, in the final analysis, it projects: *the subtlety of conceit* in a life of pretense—"The one who *makes* [feigns, pretends] to be rich" (v. 7). In the book of Proverbs (KJV) the word "conceit" occurs no less than five times (18:11; 26:5; 26:12; 26:16; 28:11). Two of these are particularly relevant to our present context. "Seest thou a man wise in his own conceit? there is more hope of a fool than of him" (26:12, KJV; see also 28:11). Egotism and pretense are the epitome of folly; hence this subtlety of conceit. But with the subtlety of conceit, there is the *penalty of conceit* in a life of pretense—"There is one *who makes himself* rich, *yet has nothing*" (v. 7). Taking the whole text in its flow, John MacArthur comments: "The same pretense is presented in two contrasting weaknesses; one pretends to be rich, while the other pretends to be poor. In contrast, men should be honest and unpretentious" (Study Bible, p. 894). The penalty for conceit is spelled out in Proverbs 18:11. In contrast to the high tower of safety which God provides for the righteous (see 18:10), "the rich man's wealth is his strong city, and as an high wall in his own conceit" (18:11, KJV). The rich man imagines that his wealth is an unassailable defense in the storms of life. But this is the penalty of conceit. What a warning to you and me! Remember the words of Jesus, "Woe to you, . . . hypocrites! . . . for a pretense [you] make long prayers. Therefore you will receive greater condemnation" (Matt. 23:14).

The Deceit of Pretense

"There is one . . . who *makes* himself poor, yet has great riches" (v. 7). Solomon repeats his verb to maintain the concept of pretense. But here the accent is on *deceit* rather than *conceit*. It is the prophet Jeremiah who reminds us that "the heart is deceitful above all things, and desperately wicked" (17:9). If a person "makes himself" rich or poor in the eyes of others, it is extremely likely that he will, before long, *imagine* himself to be so. This inevitably leads to *the deceit of falsehood* in a life of pretense—"[He] makes himself poor" (v. 7). He lies to himself, his God, his family, and injures others in the process. But right on the heels of falsehood, there is *the deceit of fraudulence*—"[He] makes himself *poor, yet has great riches*" (v. 7). Such a person brainwashes his neighbors and, in the worst cases, induces them to run serious risks to their health and fortune. It is one of the well-attested facts of human experience that what men try to *persuade* their fellows to *think*, they come to *believe themselves*! The risen Lord addressed this state of affairs when He scolded the church of Laodicea with the words, "because you say, 'I am rich, have become wealthy, and have *need of nothing*'; and do not know that you are wretched, miserable, poor, blind, and naked" (Rev. 3:17). What a word to the church today, to *you* and *me*! This has been an unusual theme, but an inescapable fact of life. Oh, to be saved from *the peril of pretense*!

O Father of lights, with whom "there is no variation or shadow of turning";—
celestial bodies change from night to day, their lights vary in intensity and shad-

ow; but YOU remain changeless! Make me like Yourself through Your dear Son. Transform any vestige of pretense in my life into solid reality, transparency, and integrity, by the power of Your mighty Spirit—for Jesus' sake. Amen.

Backsliding

"The backslider in heart will be filled with his own ways, but a good man will be satisfied from above"
Proverbs 14:14

Backsliding

"The backslider in heart will be filled with his own ways, but a good man will be satisfied from above"
Proverbs 14:14

Proverbs 14:12-18

The state of backsliding is referred to many times in Scripture and is always indicative of spiritual declension. Our text for today is one of the most comprehensive statements on the subject of backsliding and, praise God, of recovery.

The Point of Spiritual Departure

"The backslider in heart will be filled with his *own ways*" (v. 14). For the Christian, the point of spiritual departure starts with an unguarded heart. So the Scriptures warn us to guard our hearts *by the Word of the Father*—"Your word I have hidden in my heart, that I might not sin against You!" (Ps. 119:11). When we become undisciplined with our time with God each day, and transfer our confidence to religious or material activities, we are at the point of spiritual departure. We are to guard ourselves with *the Life of the Savior*—"Christ [must] dwell in [our] hearts through faith" (Eph. 3:17). Only by the conscious and continuous presence of Christ's indwelling life can the Christian know a sanctified heart. We are to guard our hearts with *the Strength of the Spirit*—"strengthened with might through His Spirit in the *inner man*" (Eph. 3:16). By the Holy Spirit, Christ dwells in our hearts *by faith*.

The Process of Spiritual Decline

"The backslider in heart will be filled with his *own ways*" (v. 14). Once the point of departure has been reached, the decline leads to inevitable disaster. The word "backslider" means "the perverse one," and pictures the wayward sheep that goes its own way until it is lost (Isa. 53:6). The word "filled" carries the added thought of covering up by rationalizing. Backsliding Christians *lie* in their praying, their singing, their talking, and even their serving. Though they know it is wrong, they still persist. "Filled" also suggests the idea of being "satisfied with complacency." The backslider who is complacent in his/her lifestyle will be set aside in uselessness (1 Cor. 11:30-31).

The Power of Spiritual Deliverance

"A good man will be satisfied from *above*" (v. 14). Man, in and of himself, has no good in him (Rom. 3:12; 7:18). Therefore, anything good about the Christian is imparted from above (James 1:17). The apostle Paul helps us understand that it is "the goodness of God" that leads us to repentance (Rom. 2:4) and dependence (Gal. 5:22) in the believing heart. Repentance means turning, every day, from our own way back to Calvary, confessing our sins, and resolving to walk in the way of righteousness. Dependence and faithfulness are the result of knowing the goodness of God. Anything less than moment–by–moment dependence on the Lord Jesus is backsliding. But repentance and dependence are not sufficient; there must be obedience to God in everything. "Therefore consider the goodness and severity of God: on those who fell, severity; but toward you, goodness, *if you continue in His goodness*. Otherwise you also will be cut off" (Rom. 11:22). Without obedience, there is divine judgment; with obedience there is divine fulfillment. Obedience is love's response to God's purpose of grace to make us like His Son. See how this principle was demonstrated in Christ's own humanity (Heb. 5:8-9). The only antidote to backsliding is obedience.

Lord God of my Fathers, and of Your redeemed people today, I hear Your cry of compassion in times past: "Return to Me, and I will return to you." Lord, this is a call to me to return from backsliding. I will now return from anything that would mar fellowship with You. Take me, cleanse me, fill me, use me—for Jesus' sake. Amen.

Prayer

*"The Lord is far from the
wicked, but He hears the
prayer of the righteous"*
Proverbs 15:29

Prayer

"The Lord is far from the wicked, but He hears the prayer of the righteous"
Proverbs 15:29

Proverbs 15:26-33

The Bible is replete with the importance and occurrence of prayer. In Old Testament times, communion and intercession between Jehovah and His people were ritualistic but real. In the New Testament, Jesus taught His disciples by example and precept how to pray. In the Acts and the Epistles, prayer was central to the life, worship, and ministry of the church. Here, in our text for today, we find a verse relatively isolated on the subject of prayer! What does this teach us?

The Privilege of Prayer

"The Lord is far from the wicked, but He hears the prayer of the righteous" (v. 29). To emphasize the positive privilege of prayer, the divine writer starts with a negative statement: "The Lord is far from the wicked" (v. 29). The reason? "The sacrifice of the wicked is an abomination to the Lord" (v. 8). Even a new convert knew this when he affirmed, "We know that God does not hear sinners; but if anyone is a worshiper of God and does His will, He hears him" (John 9:31; compare Psalm 145:18-19). Having made that point, the Holy Spirit teaches us two wonderful truths about the privilege of prayer. The first is the privilege of *divine relationship in prayer*—"The prayer of the *righteous*" (v. 29). The word "righteous" refers to "one who has been made righteous, lawful, or just, in a moral or forensic sense." And this is precisely what God has done for you and me through the merits of Christ's work on the cross. Now we enjoy the privilege of divine relationship in prayer. The second truth is the privilege of *divine responsiveness in prayer*—"The Lord … *hears* the prayer of the righteous" (v. 29). Here is both the mystery and glory of the believer's prayer-life! God *hears* (literally—"attends," "answers") our prayers. So we can say: "What a Friend we have in Jesus, all our sins and griefs to bear! What a privilege to carry everything to God in prayer!"

The Practice of Prayer

"The Lord … hears the prayer of the righteous" (v. 29). God *always* answers prayer. To interpret this amazing fact Jesus taught, "Ask, and it will be given to you; seek, and you will find; knock, and it will be opened to you" (Luke 11:9). Some answers come with *assurance* in prayer—"Ask, and it will be given to you." If we ask in the name of Jesus (John 14:14), in the power of the Spirit (Rom. 8:26), and on the Word of God (John 15:7)—we receive answers. Some answers come with *persistence* in prayer—"*Seek*, and you will find" (Luke 11:9). This persistence in *seeking* takes time and testing, and often we lose patience. But God is never in a hurry! If He has a reason to delay the answer to our prayers, we simply bow to His "good and acceptable and perfect will" (Rom. 12:2). Some answers come with *resistance* in prayer—"*Knock*, and it will be given to you" (Luke 11:9). Only God can "open or shut" doors (Rev. 3:7). When Paul "pleaded *three* times" for relief from his "thorn" (literally, "stake in the flesh") his threefold request was *denied*, but the *door of grace was opened for him to endure* (see 2 Cor. 12:8-9). It was the same with Jesus in the Garden of Gethsemane with His threefold prayer (Mark 14:32-41). It may take "repeated knocking" to open the door of resistance in prayer, but the compensations of grace more than reward the prayer of faith (1 Cor. 15:10; Phil. 4:13; Col. 1:29). Repeated knocking accompanies many mentions of prayer in the Bible. This is why Jesus said, "Men always ought to pray and not lose heart" (Luke 18:1); and Paul urged us to pray "always with all prayer" (Eph. 6:18); "pray without ceasing" (1 Thess. 5:17). What a wealth of teaching from *one* verse interpreted by *one* Bible! With the disciples of old, there is only one appropriate response, "Lord, teach us to pray" (Luke 11:1).

Lord Jesus, this is also my response! Forgive my prayerlessness, my faithlessness, my thanklessness. By Your mighty Spirit, strengthen me in my weakness, instruct me in my ignorance, and startle me in my dullness, until I pray according to Your will, and Your will alone. For Jesus' sake. Amen.

Guidance

"Commit your works to the Lord, and your thoughts will be established"
Proverbs 16:3

Guidance

"Commit your works to the Lord, and your thoughts will be established"
Proverbs 16:3

Proverbs 16:1-9

One of the exciting things about our Christian life is that God has a plan for all His children (Eph. 2:10). The Bible declares that "the steps of a good man are ordered by the Lord" (Ps. 37:23); and again, "The Lord will guide you continually" (Isa. 58:11). But the path we take and the progress we make *depend* all on our willingness to "commit our works to the Lord" (v. 31).

The Personal Commitment of Our Lives to God

"Commit your works to the Lord" (16:3). The word "commit" means "to roll on someone else"! God wants us to roll on Him - who we are - our selfhood, and what we are—our servanthood, with unconditional abandon. God is interested and involved in "the works of our hands" – whether the areas are religious, domestic, or commercial. When we walk in the path of God's will with undeviating obedience, we cannot miss God's best.

The Practical Adjustment of Our Lives by God

"Commit your works to the Lord, and your thoughts [or plans] will be established" (16:3). Guidance is a very practical matter, for it involves the minutest detail of our lives. It seems inconceivable that God could be interested in every one of our requests; but He who marks the sparrow's fall and numbers the very hairs of our heads, is interested in the practical adjustments of our lives to His "good and acceptable and perfect will" (see Matt. 6:24-34; 10:29-31; Rom. 12:1-2). Wisdom is the right application of knowledge. It is one thing to have the facts before us, but we need divine wisdom for making the right decisions. It is important, therefore, to observe and obey the will of God—to know divine guidance. Our daily prayer should be, "Guide me with Your counsel" (Ps. 73:24).

The Purposeful Fulfillment of Our Lives in God

"Commit your works to the Lord, and your thoughts [plans] will be established" (16:3). There is a threefold fulfillment in a guided life. *There is the ful-*

fillment of peace (see Ps. 119:165). There is nothing more settling and restful than to know the confirmation of God's law and will in our lives. When peace becomes our guardian against all the attempts of the enemy to dissuade us from doing the will of God, there is a blessed sense of fulfillment (see Col. 3:15). *There is the fulfillment of pleasure* (see Rom. 12:1-2). There is nothing more pleasurable than doing the will of God. Like Jesus, our consuming passion should be to do the will of God (see John 4:34; 8:29). *There is the fulfillment of purpose* (Rom 8:28). In His providence, God orchestrates every event in life, including trials, temptations, and triumphs, to accomplish His purpose in our lives. That purpose, ultimately, is conformity to Christ (Rom. 8:29). This peace, pleasure, and purpose can only be found within the parameters of a God-guided life. So let the language of our heart be, "This is God ... He will be our *guide* even to death" (Ps. 48:14).

Guide me, O my great Jehovah, pilgrim through this barren land: I am weak, but You are mighty, hold me with Your powerful hand. Keep me ever within the boundaries of Your perfect will. May I know Your guidance day by day. You have declared in Your Word, that I am created in Christ Jesus for good works which You have prepared beforehand that I should walk in them. May I daily find, follow, and finish the plan You have for my life. Answer my prayer, dear Lord. Amen.

Cheerfulness

"A merry heart does good, like medicine, but a broken spirit dries the bones"
Proverbs 17:22

Cheerfulness

"A merry heart does good, like medicine, but a broken spirit dries the bones"
Proverbs 17:22

Proverbs 17:22-28

Cheerfulness is both described and defined in our text. Cheerfulness means good courage, good cheer, and is used only in the imperative mood. If you and I are not living cheerfully, we are living disobediently!

Cheerfulness Calls for the Life of Spiritual Radiance

"A merry heart does good, like medicine" (17:22). The heart is the spring and source of all action. Therefore, to get the heart right is to get the life right. God always starts from the center and works out to the circumference of human experience. An examination of the Word of God reveals what makes a cheerful heart. *Radiance emanates from a heart that knows divine purity*. Jesus said, "Blessed are the pure in heart, for they shall see God" (Matt. 5:8). Cheerfulness and sinfulness cannot coexist. To have our hearts purified by faith implies that through faith in the Lord Jesus, we can know purity of heart. This is not only an initial experience, but a continual one. Day by day we need to be cleansed, if we are to know the blessedness and cheerfulness of a radiant life (1 John 1:9). *Radiance emanates from a heart that knows divine unity*. David prays, "I will walk in Your truth; Unite my heart to fear Your name. I will praise You, O Lord my God, with all my heart, And I will glorify Your name forevermore" (Ps. 86:11-12). This is the true secret of a life of divine radiance. No one can know cheerfulness while there is division within the heart, and to know true integration there must be the uniting power of the Lord Jesus within. *Radiance emanates from a heart that knows a divine melody*. Writing to the Ephesians believers, Paul says, "Be filled with the Spirit, speaking to one another in psalms and hymns and spiritual songs, singing and making melody in your heart to the Lord" (5:18-19). When the heart knows divine purity and unity there is always melody. The Holy Spirit fills a life that is not only separated from sin but dedicated to God.

Cheerfulness Calls for the Life of Spiritual Influence

"A merry heart does good, like medicine, but a broken spirit dries the bones" (17:22). No one can enjoy a life of spiritual radiance without effecting both an internal and an external influence. This is not only taught in our text, but it is also a fact of life. *The influence of cheerfulness is internally remedial.* A life of sorrow and misery induce a morbid condition. This is unhealthy, because man is not meant to be a perpetual incarnation of pain. On the other hand, the natural merriment of children is not only innocent, it is positively helpful to the healthy growth of their minds (see Prov. 14:30). What is true naturally is equally true spiritually. Cheerful Christians are strong Christians; they experience a life of interrelated harmony of spirit, soul, and body. *The influence of cheerfulness is externally congenial.* Congeniality is the secret of healthy and happy orientation to the changing vicissitudes of life (see Prov. 15:30). The most ill-adjusted people are those who go around creating unfriendliness and resentment because of their unhappy dispositions, and this is also a contradiction of our Christian message and testimony. On the other hand, our Christian cheerfulness should be conspicuous, continuous, and contagious!

Blessed Lord, the word "cheer" was ever on Your lips, and always in Your eyes. People left Your Presence uplifted, encouraged, and renewed. Except for a synthetic mockery of this God-given quality, we are bereft of true "cheerfulness" in the world today. Infuse me, therefore, with heaven-born cheerfulness, both as a disposition and discipline, I ask this for Your dear name's sake. Amen.

friendship

"A man who has friends must himself be friendly, but there is a friend who sticks closer than a brother"
Proverbs 18:24

Friendship

"A man who has friends must himself be friendly, but there is a friend who sticks closer than a brother"
Proverbs 18:24

Proverbs 18:19-24

Of all the gifts that God has lavished upon the human race, none is more precious than that of friendship. He created us with capacities to receive and reciprocate the joys and duties of friendship—with Himself and with our fellow men and women. As we shall see from today's text, sin has marred this holy relationship; but through our Lord Jesus, "a friend of . . . sinners" (Luke 7:34), true friendship must be found and formed only in Christ.

True Friendship must Be Found

"A man who has friends must himself *be friendly*" (v. 24). The margin reads: "A man who has *friends* may come to ruin" (v. 24), and the word for "friends" is really "companions," and carries a negative connotation. There are so–called "friends" who are no good. The pretense, or deception of friendship, must be detected and avoided. The Bible teaches and history bears out that *easy* friendship can be *evil* friendship. As we search for true friendship, we must "make no friendship with an angry man, and with a furious man [we must] not go. Lest [we] learn his ways and set a snare for [our] soul" (Prov. 22:24-25). Here are two important warnings: first, we must look for *the trait of intolerance*—"make no friendship with an angry man" (22:24). "Can two walk together, unless they are agreed?" (Amos 3:3). That is the big question at *every* level of true friendship. Secondly, we must look for *the trait of influence*—"lest [we] learn his ways and set a snare for [our] soul" (22:25). We can never underestimate the power of influence. Only in Christ can evil influence be neutralized and wholesome influence be mobilized to transform character into the likeness of Jesus.

True Friendship must Be Formed

"There is a friend who *sticks closer* than a brother" (v. 24). Our key word here is the verb "to stick closer." It suggests "to cleave" and "to cling." We often say that "blood is thicker than water," but there is a friendship which transcends even family relationships: it is the union and communion that is found and forged in Jesus Christ. He is both our Friend and Brother (John 15:14;

Heb. 2:11) through faith in Him. From that "faith-bonding" it is our joy to "cleave and cling" to Him forever. But there is more. The word "friend" in the second half of our text translates "lover." Love is never static; it is always active. So we have *the growing loyalty of love* in friendship: "Faithful are the wounds of a friend" (Prov. 27:6). A friend only hurts in order to heal. "The best Friend is the One who knows the worst about us, and loves us just the same; there's only One Who loves like that, and Jesus is His Name." We also have *the growing liberty of love* in friendship. The English root for friend is *frēon* – freedom. Jesus says to us, "No longer do I call you servants [slaves] ... I have called you friends" (John 15:15). O the "glorious liberty of the children of God" (Rom. 8:21)! Best of all, we have *the growing constancy of love* in friendship—"A friend loves at all times" (17:17). Truly, we have a Friend who sticks closer than a brother; and what is true of the transforming friendship of Jesus is carried over to "the family of friends" upon earth. This is where "the holy synergism" of saints in Christ provides the atmosphere and activity in which friendship is forged and formed as our heavenly Father intended. There is no friendship like Christian friendship!

O Friend of Abraham, Moses, and sinners like me, I trust You, I praise You, and I love You. Because You have called me Your friend, I will take time to hear the secrets of Your heart each day, and then go out to make friends for Your kingdom. This is my prayer and my pledge for Your name's sake alone. Amen.

Anger

"The discretion of a man makes him slow to anger, and his glory is to overlook a transgression"
Proverbs 19:11

Anger

"The discretion of a man makes him slow to anger, and
his glory is to overlook a transgression"
Proverbs 19:11

Proverbs 19:9-12

Wrath, anger, and indignation are an integral part of biblical revelation. In all honesty we cannot present the God of love without also declaring the God of wrath. The wrath of God is not so much an emotion or an angry frame of mind as it is a settled opposition of His holiness to evil. Therefore, if we are partakers of "the divine nature" we must be angry against sin.

There is a Time to Express Anger

"The *discretion* of a man makes him slow to anger" (v. 11). While there is a time to express anger (see Eph. 4:26), the discreet man will be slow to anger. Anger is the *divine response* to evil. This is affirmed over 300 times in Scripture. Christ displayed such holy anger when the legalists tried to trick Him with their theological stupidities, when He drove the moneychangers and religious racketeers from the temple, and when His own disciples attempted to prevent the little children from coming to Him. Anger is also the *divine defense* to evil. The Christian is instructed to become angry at evil. For example, Paul was angered by the false gods of Athens. He was angry at the power of false religion to delude the people. He was angry at the reckless devotion to powerless gods and the staggering wealth sacrificially given to build temples to honor them instead of the God of creation and redemption (see Ps. 97:10; Prov. 8:13; Rom. 12:9). Note how the apostle was "provoked" within himself when he saw the city given over to idols (Read carefully Acts 17:16-34). God give us the same revelation to demonic practices as Paul expresses in 1 Corinthians 10:19–22. We are to "be angry, and ... not sin" (Eph. 4:26).

There is a Time to Repress Anger

"The discretion of a man makes him *slow* to anger" (v. 11). To put it another way, there is a time when anger must be repressed. James points this out when he exhorts, "Let every man be swift to hear, slow to speak, slow to wrath; for the wrath of man does not produce the righteousness of God" (1:19-20). It is quite obvious from these words that there is a human quality of anger which never produces or achieves the righteousness of God. Because of this, anger must be controlled. We must ask: when is anger unrighteous? It is unrighteous when it is excited without sufficient cause, when it transcends the cause, when it is against a person rather than an offense, when it is attended with the desire for revenge, when it is cherished and heightened by reflection, and when it is accompanied by an unforgiving spirit. The victorious Christian knows how to master the chain reaction that leads to uncontrolled anger (1:19). He learns to control the thought, then the tongue, and especially the temper.

There is a Time to Redress Anger

"The discretion of a man makes him slow to anger, and his glory is to *overlook* a transgression" (v. 11). In overlooking a transgression we imitate the God of mercy and of grace. Our God is the God of redress. The word means that He compensates, makes amends, and provides a remedy. This redress must not be construed as compromise, for God never compromises; He never condones sin; but on the basis of what was accomplished at Calvary He can and does withhold His anger and extend His mercy. As His children, we must do the same. There are times when we must redress our anger. The only difference is that we must make sure that the anger that burns in our hearts does not harbor bitterness and malice.

O God of righteousness, holiness, and graciousness, enable me by Your enabling grace to "abhor what is evil, and cling to what is good"; to "be angry, and ... not sin"—that I may be salt in the earth and light in the world—through Jesus Christ my Lord. Amen.

Laziness

*"The lazy man will not plow
because of winter; he will
beg during harvest and
have nothing"*
Proverbs 20:4

Laziness

"The lazy man will not plow because of winter; he will beg during harvest and have nothing"
Proverbs 20:4

Proverbs 20:4-13

The Book of Proverbs introduces us to the sluggard and the slothful man. Laziness is the opposite of diligence and is always exposed unfavorably in Scripture. This is particularly true of the text now before us. According to this statement, the sluggard is a lazy man we must study and avoid.

The Nature of the Lazy Person

"*The lazy man will not plow* because of winter" (v. 4). Laziness is as old as human sin. Until Adam fell he possessed the unimpaired divine capacity to work, but the moment he disobeyed the voice of his Maker he incurred the penalty of death. Spiritually, he died at once; physically, he began to die; and vocationally, he experienced a deadening effect on all his labors. Ever since then man has had to conquer a vocational inertia in order to succeed in a world that favors laziness; it is part of his very nature.

The Posture of the Lazy Person

"The lazy man will not plow *because of winter*" (v. 4). The Holy Spirit is so concerned about this matter of laziness that He has given us a number of word pictures of the sluggard in the book of Proverbs. *The lazy man's posture is one of sinfulness* (18:9). Man was created by God to work; so lack of industry and too much leisure can easily lead to sin, misery, and destruction. *The lazy man's posture is one of sluggishness* (19:24; 26:15). The word "bosom" here, and in the parallel passage (26:15), is rightly rendered "dish." The lazy man's self-induced inertia prevents him from moving his hand from the dish to his mouth! He would sooner hide his hand in his bosom or armpit (alternative rendering)! The reason?—the sluggishness of his mind. He is ignorant of his ignorance (see 26:15). What a warning to those of us who fail to appropriate what God provides in those "dishes"! *The lazy man's posture is one of selfishness* (21:25-26). This means that the sluggard craves rest, pleasure, and enjoyment, but refuses to work. *The lazy man's posture is one of spinelessness* (22:13; 26:13). These two proverbs poke fun at the lazy individual who invents all sorts of excuses for avoiding work and risk. He professes to be in danger in his protected home when he *knows* that lions live in the open country! *The lazy man's posture is one of senselessness* (24:30-31). In spite of the fact that God has made us to bear the fruit of character and service, scores of people in our churches are failing to produce the fruit of the Spirit that glorifies God.

The Future of the Lazy Person

"The lazy man will not plow because of winter; *he will beg during harvest and have nothing*" (v. 4). We are essentially creatures of eternity, and whether we like it or not, we move on to an inescapable destiny. The plowing of today will be followed by the harvest of tomorrow. If we fail in our plowing we shall fail in our reaping. This is the whole thrust of our text. The life of laziness leads to bankruptcy and tragedy. A solemn word to those of us who live in dreamy unconcern about the future! The apostle Paul put it well when he wrote: "Do not be deceived, God is not mocked; for whatever a man sows, that he will also reap. For he who sows to his flesh will of the flesh reap corruption, but he who sows to the Spirit will of the Spirit reap everlasting life" (Gal. 6:7-8). This agricultural principle is applied to the moral and spiritual realms and is both universal and *personal*. It applies to *you* and *me*.

O Lord, what a lesson on laziness! Save me from this fatal disease. Fill me with Your Spirit of zeal, joy, and purpose to do Your will and work—to the end of my days! Let my prayer ever be:—"I must be about my Father's business." I ask this in Jesus' name. Amen.

Reality

"*A false witness shall perish,
but the man who hears him
will speak endlessly*"
Proverbs 21:28

Reality

"A false witness shall perish, but the man who hears him will speak endlessly"
Proverbs 21:28

Proverbs 21:21-31

Bible language is bandied about today without any notion of true content or meaningful comprehension. People talk about "born again Christians," which in the very nature of things is a ridiculous statement of redundancy. A person is a Christian because he is born again. If he is not born again he is not a Christian. Yet these terms are popularly used because of the absence of *reality* in many areas of church life. It is time that we call a halt to religious play acting and face what the Bible means by reality, as found in Jesus Christ.

We Must Renounce Synthetic Christianity

"A false witness shall perish, but the man who hears him will speak endlessly" (v. 28). A false witness is a person who is unreal or hypocritical, and therefore represents "synthetic Christianity." In the Greek, "hypocrite" means "a play actor" or "a person who acts what he really isn't." There is a sense in which all of us are play actors. We pretend to be what we are not. In the 23rd chapter of Matthew, our Lord warns of four aspects of hypocrisy. *There is a persuasiveness which is dangerous.* Jesus called hypocrites "blind guides" (Matt. 23:16). People who are blinded by their own hypocrisy are a menace because they try to lead others down the same path. *There is an impressiveness which is odious.* Jesus also called the scribes and Pharisees "whitewashed tombs" (Matt. 23:27). He was referring to tombstones that were painted each year to prevent people from touching them, and thereby defiling themselves. These tombstones were white and impressive but were full of dead men's bones. Outward appearances and expressions don't matter, if the heart is not right with God. *There is a seductiveness which is poisonous.* Jesus also described the scribes and Pharisees as deadly "serpents" (Matt. 23:33). Hypocrites betray the Savior, even though they may appear to be serving Him, and poison other people's minds as well. Ultimately, *there is a destructiveness which is serious.* Jesus warned, "How can you escape the condemnation of hell?" (Matt. 23:33). Hypocrites may have their day, but their doom is already determined; they will find their place in outer darkness.

We Must Reveal Authentic Christianity

"The man who hears ... will speak endlessly" (v. 28). Against the somber truth we have considered, we have a three-faceted jewel of positive teaching. *A real Christian has a vital faith*—"The man who hears" (v. 28). The verb means "to hear intelligently"; and Jesus reminds us that "everyone who is of the truth hears My voice" (John 18:37). The evidence of vital faith is the ability to hear and to obey divine truth. *A true Christian has a vocal faith*—"A man who hears ... will speak" (v. 28). A Christian who does not confess his faith is a contradiction! This is why the early Christians—even under severe persecution—had to confess, "We cannot but speak the things which we have seen and heard" (Acts 4:20). It is a basic principle that "out of the abundance of the heart the mouth speaks" (Matt. 12:34). *A real Christian has a visual faith*— "The man who hears ... will speak endlessly [constantly, KJV]" (v. 28). The word "endlessly" or "constantly" derives from a Hebrew word which literally means "to glitter from afar" or "to be eminent." What a suggestive concept! The *real* Christian has a quality of life that affirms what he is as well as what he says. He glitters from afar! He carries about him that divine aura of eminence. As believers, we are to "become blameless and harmless, children of God without fault in the midst of a crooked and perverse generation, among whom [we] shine as lights in the world" (Phil. 2:15). God make us real, real, real!

Almighty and everlasting Father, I know that "You desire truth in the inward parts," and reality in the outward life. Preserve me from synthetic Christianity, and produce in me authentic Christianity—that the world may believe that I belong to You. I pray this in the strong name of Jesus. Amen.

Parenthood

"Train up a child in the way he should go, and when he is old he will not depart from it"
Proverbs 22:6

Parenthood

"Train up a child in the way he should go, and when he is old he will not depart from it"
Proverbs 22:6

Proverbs 22:1-6

There is a sense in which we never leave school. The whole of life is a campus where we are being trained and fitted for eternity. As fathers and mothers we largely determine the direction and destiny of our children. With this in mind we need to examine afresh the principles that are involved in bringing up children "in the training and admonition of the Lord" (Eph. 6:4).

The Age for Parenting Our Children

"Train up a child" (Prov. 22:6). Childhood is the proper period for schooling. The divine laws that God has laid down hold good for all countries and at all times. Solomon says, "Remember now your Creator in the days of your youth, before the difficult days come, and the years draw near when you say, 'I have no pleasure in them'" (Eccles. 12:1). According to the wise man, childhood is the age of greatest impressions, innocence, and interest.

The Art of Parenting Our Children

"*Train* up a child in the way he should go" (v. 6). The Hebrew literally reads: "Initiate a child in accordance with *his way*." "His way" means one of two things: either his future calling and station, or his character and vocational inclination. There is an element of truth in both these views. Ultimately, there is only one right way: it is God's way—a way that is specified in great detail in the book of Proverbs and the rest of Scripture. John MacArthur points out that, "Since it is axiomatic that early training secures lifelong habits, parents must insist upon this way, teaching God's Word" (The MacArthur Study Bible, p. 908). We must remember that this proverb is not a promise; it is a statement of principle—which God has laid down for all parents and teachers who have the awesome responsibility of affecting little lives for all eternity. Training includes teaching, but teaching does not necessarily include training. The Bible analyzes this word "train" in a threefold manner. In its context, training includes and involves demonstration (example), education, and castigation (see Eph. 6:1-4). The Scriptures insist that all such training must have a *Christian basis.*

The Aim of Parenting Our Children

"Train up a child in the way he should go" (22:6). There is only one right way of life, and that is the way which God has made known to men and women through Jesus Christ His Son. It is the way of *salvation.* The Savior speaks of "these little ones who believe in Me" (Matt. 18:6); and from a child Timothy knew the Scriptures which were "able to make [him] wise for salvation through faith which is in Christ Jesus" (2 Tim. 3:15). The aim of parenting is also the way of *satisfaction.* The phrase "the way he should go" can also be translated "in His way," suggesting that, for every child, God has a special plan and purpose (see Eph. 2:10). What is more satisfying to a child, parent, and teacher than to know that a young life is fulfilling the very purpose for which God created him? The aim of parenting finally leads to the way of *service* as God has planned. As parents, we should teach our children what is the "whole duty of man" (Eccles. 12:13). Jesus put it this way, "It is written, 'You shall worship the Lord your God, and Him *only* you shall *serve*'" (Matt. 4:10).

Lord God, Your holy Word instructs parents to teach their children in all the ways of Your divine will; to lay these divine words upon their hearts and souls. Such language convicts me when I think of the superficial way most parents go about doing this today. Use this devotional to give me and all who read it a new concept and conviction on parenthood and parenting; for Your dear name's sake. Amen.

Truth

"Buy the truth, and do not sell it, also wisdom and instruction and understanding"
Proverbs 23:23

Truth

*"Buy the truth, and do not sell it, also wisdom and
instruction and understanding"*
Proverbs 23:23

Proverbs 23:19-26

Augustine affirmed that the Word, Jesus Christ, is Truth because He
expresses the Father. Therefore, our aim as Christians is to give ourselves
to truth as it is found in Jesus Christ. Paul called it "the excellence of the
knowledge of Christ Jesus [our] Lord" (Phil. 3:8).

We Must Price the Truth

"Buy the truth" (v. 23). Truth is *absolute*, so how do you price it? The answer is awesome. We can only price truth in terms of our infinite God as Father, Son, and Holy Spirit. As Father, God represents the *purity* of truth. In His High Priestly Prayer Jesus could request His Father with these words, "Sanctify them by Your truth. Your word is truth" (John 17:17). No words could express more powerfully the confidence of Jesus in the veracity and sanctity of truth. As Son, God represents the *pattern* of truth. Only one Person could stand on planet earth and declare with majestic authority, "I am … the truth" (John 14:6). Since truth is essentially moral, only one Person in the universe could embody and express eternal truth in human form. As Holy Spirit, God represents the *power* of truth. Jesus described the third person of the Trinity as "The Spirit of truth" (John 16:13). This is how we must adjust our minds, hearts, and wills as we price the truth; and this is essential if we are to "buy the truth" (v. 23).

We Must Purchase the Truth

"Buy the truth, and … also wisdom and instruction and understanding" (v. 23). Truth will never yield its treasures without "blood, sweat, and tears." Such effort calls for *deployment of time*. This is implied and involved in acquiring "wisdom"—practical knowledge; "instruction"—moral culture and discipline; "understanding"—the use of the faculty of discernment. With deployment of time, there must be the *discipline of truth*—"Do not sell [truth]" (v. 23)—it is precious, it is profitable, and most important, it is personal. In the language of the apostle Paul we must "be diligent to present [ourselves] approved to God, a worker who does not need to be ashamed, rightly dividing the word of truth" (2 Tim. 2:15).

We Must Protect the Truth

"And do not *sell* it" (v. 23). The Bible says that "we can do nothing against the truth, but for the truth" (2 Cor. 13:8). What we think or do about truth does not affect the truth, in and of itself. However, we can deny, distort, or dilute the truth by the way we misrepresent it. This is a cardinal sin. So we are exhorted to "[hold] fast the faithful word" (Titus 1:9); to "[strive] together for the faith of the gospel" (Phil. 1:27); and "to contend earnestly for the faith which was once for all delivered to the saints" (Jude 3). We must guard against the personal exaggeration, popular accommodation, poisonous contamination of truth. With the apostle Paul we must be able to stand up and affirm, " I am appointed for the defense of the gospel" (Phil. 1:17). And with "Jude, a servant of Jesus Christ" we must share the burden of "our common salvation" and "contend earnestly for the faith which was once for all delivered to the saints" (Jude 3).

Lord Jesus, You are TRUTH. How can I understand this mind-boggling fact and be neutral about truth? Indeed, dear Lord, the crisis of the modern hour is about truth. That is what postmodernism is all about. Truth is God the Father, truth is God the Son, and truth is God the Holy Spirit. I am for truth, or not for truth; there is no alternative for me. Do or die, I am for truth now and forever. Amen.

Humanity

"Rescue those being led away to death; hold back those staggering toward slaughter. If you say, 'But we knew nothing about this.' Does not he who weighs the heart perceive it? Does not he who guards your life know it? Will he not repay each person according to what he has done?"
Proverbs 24:11-12, NIV

Humanity

"Rescue those being led away to death; hold back those staggering toward slaughter. If you say, 'But we knew nothing about this.' Does not he who weighs the heart perceive it? Does not he who guards your life know it? Will he not repay each person according to what he has done?"
Proverbs 24:11-12, NIV

Proverbs 24:11-12

There is such a thing as *the law of humanity* in the moral universe in which we live. People around us cannot suffer and die, as if it did not *matter*. The fact that God has made us in His image means that we can think, feel, and act. Therefore, human relationships *must* concern us, whether we like it or not.

Our Human Dependability Matters in the Relationships of Life

"Rescue those being led away to death; hold back those staggering toward slaughter" (v. 12, NIV). These words of divine mandate presuppose human dependability whenever "duty calls or danger." For the Christian, this dependability means *social concern*. There is hardly a page in the Gospels where human rights are not commended, and abused privileges not condemned and judged (see Matt. 25:31-46). The recurring emphasis of our Lord in His teaching suggests that the believer must be prepared to forego his own rights as long as those less fortunate are advanced. Having stressed social concern, we must not overlook *spiritual compassion*. The Scriptures maintain a balance between physical and spiritual needs. Just as the Messiah visited people for the purpose of redemption (see Luke 1:68,78), so we must visit men and women in spiritual need around us (see James 1:27).

Our Human Responsibility Matters in the Relationships of Life

"If you say, 'But we knew nothing about this,' does not he who weighs the heart perceive it? Does not he who guards your life know it?" (v. 12, NIV). For human dependability to operate, there must be human responsibility. Men and women have been making excuses from the beginning, but God does not let us off the hook; He knows our hearts and reads our motives. We are responsible for the ignorance that fails to *see* human need. We live in a world where human need is like an open book, so there is no excuse for ignorance. We are also responsible for the indifference that fails to *sense* human need. If there is indifference to human responsibility then there must be *heart* trouble on our part.

Our Human Accountability Matters in the Relationships of Life

"Will [God] not repay each person according to what he has done?" (v. 12, NIV). A repeated theme throughout Scripture is our accountability, in the day of reckoning, for what we have done, or failed to do, in relation to the people we have touched along life's journey. Jesus talked about this day of reckoning when He described the Son of man coming in all His glory, and setting up His throne of judgment, commending the faithful and condemning those who had failed their duty (Matt. 25:34-46). Read carefully the Lord's worldview of struggling humanity (Matt. 9:35-38). Read also Paul's concern for His own people (Rom. 9:1-5). If you don't care—turn to Ezekiel 33 and study verses 1-11.

Lord Jesus, forgive me for being so insensitive to humanity's need all around me. It is so easy and glib to stand up in public and preach about love and yet be so loveless and careless when it comes to my family, my neighbors, and a lost world! Break me, melt me, mold me, and fill me with Calvary love. I pray this for Your glory alone. Amen.

Communi-cation

"A word fitly spoken is like apples of gold in settings of silver"
Proverbs 25:11

Communication

"A word fitly spoken is like apples of gold in settings of silver"
Proverbs 25:11

Proverbs 25:11

Our God is a God of self-disclosure, revealing Himself in all the glory of His person, power, and purpose. He is supremely a communicator. His full and final revelation was personified in Jesus Christ His Son (see Heb. 1:1-2). Christ's purpose in coming into the world was twofold: to make us Christians and to make us communicators. As communicators, we have a message to share.

Our Message must be Verbalized

"A word fitly spoken" (v. 11). In order to communicate with men, God "became flesh and dwelt among us, and we beheld His glory, the glory as of the only begotten of the Father, full of grace and truth" (John 1:14). By life and by lip Jesus communicated the mind of God; it was the "word fitly spoken." Eternal truth was verbalized in terms that men and women could understand. Verbalization requires an *appropriate* word. In the Hebrew "a word fitly spoken" means "a word spoken in season," and can be rendered "a word spoken according to the circumstances." The appropriate word is real and relevant. Verbalization also requires an *articulate* word. In the Master's articulation there was clarity and artistry, and He calls us to the same.

Our Message must be Vitalized

"A word fitly spoken" (v. 11). The term translated "fitly" in the original Hebrew signifies "wheels." This is why the margin reads, "A word spoken on wheels." When words leave the mouth they should be like a vehicle on easygoing wheels. This suggests *dynamic motion* in communication. We will never reach our generation unless we communicate with words on wheels. The secret, of course, is the mighty anointing of the Spirit. It is significant that when the apostles were filled with the Holy Spirit they "spoke the word of God with boldness" (Acts 4:31). But there must also be a *specific mission* in communication. When God sent His Son to be the incarnate Word He came with a mission, and having completed the mission He said to His disciples, "As the Father has sent Me, I also send you" (John 20:21). Whether in conversation or proclamation, our mission is to make known the gospel of our Lord Jesus Christ.

Our Message must be Visualized

"A word fitly spoken is like *apples of gold in settings of silver*" (v. 11). This is a picture of oriental beauty. The finely turned metaphor is chosen by the writer to give the highest possible praise to the "word fitly spoken." The emphasis is clearly on that which is visual or pictorial. This is an essential element in the art of communication. *There must be color in our presentation of truth*. Truth should be colorful, attractive, and appealing. In terms of verbal communication, our preaching and soul-winning should be illustrative and incarnational. *There must be content in our presentation of truth*. The implication of presenting apples in a setting of silver is significant. You do not normally put what is worthless in silver; on the contrary, you put in the valuable apples of gold. This speaks of content, and that is what communication is all about. Paul exhorted Timothy to "preach the word" (2 Tim. 4:2). Ultimately, the secret of redemptive preaching is "fleshing out" in living color the indwelling Christ by the power of the Holy Spirit. Unless we are visual, we cannot be vital "apples of gold in settings of silver!"

Lord Jesus, make me an effective communicator of Your blessed Self. This is why You have saved and sent me. Never let me speak unless I am consciously filled and anointed with Your Holy Spirit. May I be characterized by content, color, and most importantly, Christlikeness. For Your dear name's sake. Amen.

Retribution

"Whoever digs a pit will fall into it, and he who rolls a stone will have it roll back on him"
Proverbs 26:27

Retribution

"Whoever digs a pit will fall into it, and he who rolls a stone will have it roll back on him"
Proverbs 26:27

Proverbs 26:26-28

This proverb is of such significance and importance that it also occurs, in almost identical words, in the books of Psalms and Ecclesiastes. At first glance, it might not arrest our attention. After all, there is nothing unusual about digging pits and rolling stones; but on closer examination solemn principles emerge. Here, in small compass, is taught the doctrine of *retribution*.

The Law of Retribution Reveals
the Foulness of Man's Degradation

"Whoever digs a pit will fall into it, and he who rolls a stone will have it roll back on him" (v. 27). In proverbial language, we have here the techniques by which man's inhumanity to man is perpetrated. *There is a degraded subtlety which controls people*—"Whoever digs a pit" (v. 27). The Bible reminds us that when Satan traps his victim he does so through subtlety (see Gen. 3:1). This satanic subtlety has continued to manifest itself in men and women throughout the centuries. The metaphor of the pit in this verse illustrates this. The pits were dug to catch wild animals. They were shaped so that the aperture was small enough to hide or camouflage with light branches, leaves and scattered earth, and the sides were slanted outward and downward so as to make it virtually impossible to climb out. As we look around us today, there are pits being dug everywhere—in international, national, and personal life. There is something in our depraved natures that propels us to dig pits for others. There is a fiendish delight to see our victims struggling. In spite of the law of retribution we persist in pit digging. *There is a degraded cruelty which crushes people*—"He who rolls a stone" (v. 27). This does not refer to throwing stones into the air, which fall upon the head of the thrower, but to rolling stones up to a given height in order to hurl them down upon the enemy (i.e., Judges 9:53; 2 Sam. 11:21). There is nothing complicated about this practice; it is brazen and brutal. Again, we see stones being rolled in international, national, and personal life today.

The Law of Retribution Reflects
the Fairness of God's Intervention

"Whoever digs a pit will fall into it, and he who rolls a stone will have it roll back on him" (v. 27). Jesus enunciated the same principle when He declared, "For with what judgment you judge, you will be judged; and with the measure you use, it will be measured back to you" (Matt. 7:2). *There is often a present retribution.* The Bible says, "Be sure your sin will find you out" (Num. 32:23). Thus God does take "the wise in their own craftiness" (1 Cor. 3:19) and the wicked in his wickedness (see Prov. 11:5; Ezek. 18:20). *There is always a future retribution.* There are many warnings in the Bible concerning eternal retribution. The doctrine has been held and taught by Christians since the days of the apostles. They believed the Bible taught that the impenitent will be cast into hell, from which there is no escape. This punishment is likened in many places to a pit (Num. 16:32-33; Rev. 20:1-3), "the gates of Sheol" (Job 17:16), the "lake of fire burning with brimstone" (Rev. 19:20). How solemn to recognize that those who dig pits today could find themselves in the pit of eternal darkness and separation from God. The man or woman who rolls a stone up a hill in order to hurl it at others will one day be crushed by that very stone. The action of such a person is an evidence of his or her *rejection of Christ.* The point is that there is a day of retribution (Acts 17:31).

Holy God, because You are a God of love, righteousness, and judgment, You have erected warning signs throughout Your Word—from cover to cover. Thank

You for this warning word today. It has challenged my mind, heart, and will; may it do the same to all who read this devotional. Amen and Amen.

Futurity

"Do not boast about tomorrow, for you do not know what a day may bring forth. Let another man praise you, and not your own mouth; a stranger, and not your own lips"
Proverbs 27:1-2

Futurity

"Do not boast about tomorrow, for you do not know what a day may bring forth. Let another man praise you, and not your own mouth; a stranger, and not your own lips"
Proverbs 27:1-2

Proverbs 27:1-2

Few things in life concern us more than the fear of the future. Recognizing this, the Lord Jesus said, "Do not worry or be anxious about tomorrow, for tomorrow will have worries and anxieties of its own. Sufficient for each day is its own trouble" (Matt. 6:34, Amplified N.T.). Where there is a will to live we do our utmost to ensure a future of prosperity and security. On the other hand, when hope is gone we write our wills and prepare for our departure. In short, there is a future which we cannot—and dare not—ignore.

We must Face the Future with Sensitive Caution

"Do not boast about tomorrow" (v. 1). Life is so uncertain that no one can predict the future. In view of this, our text cautions us about *a boastful arrogance*. To boast is to brag or praise one's self, and God cautions against this. In Luke 12:16-21 we have the story of a man who personified this arrogance. In fewer than three verses he uses the pronoun "I" five times. Because of man's fallenness, self was the great and ultimate object of his glorying. The farmer boasted of his wealth (Luke 12:17) and his health (Luke 12:19). All he could see was a prosperous future with plenty to eat, drink, and enjoy. God's answer to such boastfulness is both swift and solemn! The Greek rendering of verse 20 is impressive, "This night *they* require your soul." Most likely the "they" are the angels whose special function is to conduct the souls of the departed to their own place (Luke 16:22). Such a story, then, cautions us against boastful arrogance, but we are also cautioned against a *blissful ignorance*. While our Lord tells us not to worry about the future, He certainly does not encourage blissful ignorance. The message of the Bible is, "Prepare to meet your God" (Amos 4:12). This calls for an educated mental attitude toward all that we do know about the future. We cannot remain in a state of blissful ignorance when God's Word is plain, "Do not boast about tomorrow, for you do not know what a day may bring forth" (v. 1).

We must Face the Future with Positive Action

"Do not boast about tomorrow, for you do not know what a day may bring forth" (v. 1). The negative is stressed here to inspire a positive call to action. This demands a life of *humility*. The antidote to boastfulness is a life of humbleness. The prophet Micah sums it up when he says, "What does the Lord require of you but to do justly, to love mercy, and to walk humbly with your God?" (6:8). In the New Testament we learn that this humility is both a disposition that God entrusts to us and a discipline that God expects from us. This discipline calls for self-denial and daily cross-bearing. No one can live this life of humility and be boastful. We are also called to a life of *dependency*. When the Lord Jesus cautioned His disciples about worrying over the future, He preceded His exhortation with two glorious affirmations. He declared, "For your heavenly Father *knows*" and "your heavenly Father *feeds*" (Matt. 6:32, 26). Our God is the God of *prevision* as well as *provision*. Nothing can ever happen to us without His previous knowledge. No need can ever occur in our lives for which He is not more than adequate. Finally, the call to action demands a life of *activity*. The first two verses of this chapter are connected in both spirit and subject. As we face the future with positive action, a life of humility and dependency will lead to activity—and such activity will either call forth our Master's praise of the "well done" or our Master's rebuke of "slothful servant." The supreme ambition of our lives should be to live and serve to the glory of God, as our Savior did (see Luke 2:49; John 4:34; 8:29; 9:4).

Dear Lord, a couplet that changed my life forever comes to mind as I write this prayer: "Only one life 'twill soon be past, only what's done for Christ will last." A framed copy hangs in my study to remind me every day. Hang it in my heart and in every heart that reads this prayer; for Your dear name's sake. Amen.

Trans-
parency

*"He who covers his sin will
not prosper, but whoever confesses and forsakes them will
have mercy"*
Proverbs 28:13

Transparency

*"He who covers his sin will not prosper, but whoever
confesses and forsakes them will have mercy"*
Proverbs 28:13

Proverbs 28:11-14

God made man to walk in light. That is why Christians are called "children of light" (Eph. 5:8). The theme of the Bible since that first tragic fall in the Garden of Eden has been man's restoration to fellowship with God. He loves the creatures of His hand and longs to fellowship with them in light (see 1 John 1:5-10). The life of transparency is viewed in our text from three angles.

The Folly of Deceitfulness

"He who covers his sin will not prosper" (v. 13). The Bible reminds us that "if we say that we have no sin, we deceive ourselves, and the truth is not in us" (1 John 1:8). Inherent in every one of us is the propensity to sin and cover up. There is *the practice of deceitfulness*. There are various as well as devious ways in which sinners and saints conceal their wrongdoing: excuses, exploitation, and even enjoyment! But all such deceitfulness is futile because "God requires an account of what is past" (Eccles. 3:15). There is also *the peril of deceitfulness*, for whatever the outward appearances may seem to be, the deceitful person is headed for serious trouble. Such a person lives a lie, and God hates hypocrisy (see Matt. 23:13-36). For another thing, such a life of deceitfulness precludes forgiveness. God only pardons the penitent, and such penitence is impossible without an admission of guilt. What is even worse, the practice of deceitfulness confirms the sinner in his sin. Sin is never destroyed by being covered, it will spring forth in an even greater harvest of evil.

The Duty of Disclosure

"He who covers his sins will not prosper, but whoever confesses and forsakes them will have mercy" (v. 13). Confessing and forsaking sin are more than good therapy; they are divine requirements. This duty of disclosure is twofold: *sin must be admitted*. Confession of sin is *personal* (1 John 1:9). It has to do with one's own fellowship with God. Whenever sin interrupts that fellowship there should be no delay in confessing the sin and seeking restored fellowship. Confession is also *social* (Matt. 6:14-15). Until we put relationships right between ourselves and our brother, we can never expect God to hear or bless us. Confession is also *general* (Matt. 18:15-18). This is when wrongdoing affects the whole church. *Sin must be abandoned* (Matt. 18:15-18). True confession must be accompanied by repentance. Without such renunciation of sin our approach to God for forgiveness and cleansing is sheer mockery. Forsaking sin involves action and apology. At other times it calls for reconciliation and restitution.

The Glory of Deliverance

"He who . . . confesses and forsakes [his sins] will have *mercy*" (v. 13). The mercy of God is one of the great themes of biblical revelation. In His mercy we find the glory of deliverance for men and women who are prepared to confess and forsake their sins. This glorious deliverance comes through *the mercy of the Father's pardon* (Isa. 55:7). Because of the atoning sacrifice of the Lord Jesus Christ, God can have mercy upon us and "abundantly pardon" all who are prepared to confess and forsake their sins. Deliverance also comes through *the mercy of the Savior's presence* (Heb. 4:16). There is a sense in which the Lord Jesus never leaves us or forsakes us, so we can "come boldly to the throne of grace, that we may obtain mercy, and find grace to help in time of need." There is also deliverance through *the mercy of the Spirit's power* (Titus 3:5). The initial and continual power to live the Christian life is enabled by the Holy Spirit resulting in growth and good works. But notice carefully how the Spirit's power is linked with divine mercy. This power enables us to live and serve to the glory of God.

Lord Jesus, it is only by Your mercy that I can frame this prayer. By nature and by choice I want to sin—and then cover it up. And I have proved again and again that I do not prosper. But I praise You that because of the Father's pardon, the Savior's presence, and the Spirit's power, I can know transformation and transparency through divine mercy in my life. Hallelujah! Amen!

Vision

"Where there is no vision, the people perish: but he that keepeth the law, happy is he"
Proverbs 29:18

Vision

"Where there is no vision, the people perish: but he that keepeth the law, happy is he"
Proverbs 29:18

Proverbs 29:18-27

The word "vision" occurs some 31 times in the Old Testament and denotes that which is communicated by God to man through prophetic preaching. In the context of today's verse, it refers to the prophetic vision of God as related to man's needs. The inspired writer tells us that without this anointed preaching "the people perish," or "become naked," or "cast off restraint."

The Absence of Vision

"Where there is no vision, the people perish" (v. 18, KJV). As the salt of the earth, God's people are expected to arrest corruption, and as the light of the world they are commanded to dispel darkness. But "where there is no vision" the reverse happens: *people become spiritually defenseless*—when they turn their eyes from God they become vulnerable to the attacks of the enemy; *people become naturally defiant*—when they cease to "retain God in their knowledge" (Rom. 1:28ff.), God gives them up to a "debased mind"; *people become personally destructive*—as they lose faith in divine revelation, they are filled with all "unrighteousness, sexual immorality, wickedness, covetousness, maliciousness; full of envy, murder" (Rom. 1:29).

The Presence of Vision

"Where there is no vision, the people perish: but he that keepeth the law, happy is he" (v. 18, KJV). Where and when God's people are prepared to see and heed divine revelation, there is a reversal of the sequence of moral deterioration. Prophetic vision produces *redemptive passion*. When Jesus "saw the multitudes, He was moved with compassion for them, because they were weary [harassed] and scattered, like sheep having no shepherd" (Matt. 9:36). This redemptive passion leads to *responsive action*. Having looked out on the multitudes Jesus said to His disciples: "The harvest truly is plentiful, but the laborers are few. Therefore pray the Lord of the harvest to send out laborers into His harvest" (Matt. 9:37-38). Read further and you will find that these disciples were the answer to their own prayer. This is the best outworking of true *vision!* To have this redemptive concern slays all selfishness, laziness, and carelessness in us and sends us forth to seek and to save that which is lost. Redemptive passion always leads to *responsive action*; vision begets venture. James encourages us to be "doers of the word, and not hearers only" (1:22).

The Essence of Vision

"Where there is no vision, the people perish: but he that keepeth the law, happy is he" (v. 18, KJV). In the parallelism employed here are two words of comprehensive significance. One is *law*—which for our purpose is the *revelation* of the Word of God; and the other is *vision* which corresponds to the *inspiration* of the Spirit of God. These two essentials of God's prophetic actions were powerfully demonstrated on the Day of Pentecost in fulfillment of Joel's prophecy (see Joel 2:28-32). When God's *Spirit* is poured upon "all flesh," "young men see visions"; "old men dream dreams." In obedience to the Word of God and the Spirit of God there is this balanced result: God combines the spiritual acuity of young people with the spiritual maturity of old men. This is the essence of vision! Acuity without maturity would lead to imbalance; and maturity without acuity would lead to impatience! Show me the combination of these two mighty forces and I will show you a church that has vision!

Lord Jesus, thank You for opening up this amazing verse for me. You have shown me what "no vision" means—chaotic disaster! But You have also shown me what real vision means—dynamic deliverance! Combine in me spiritual maturity and spiritual acuity. I pray this in Jesus' name. Amen!

Stateliness

"There are three things that are stately in their stride, four that move with stately bearing; a lion, mighty among beasts, who retreats before nothing; a strutting rooster, a he-goat, and a king with his army around him"
Proverbs 30:29-31, NIV

Stateliness

"There are three things that are stately in their stride, four that move with stately bearing; a lion, mighty among beasts, who retreats before nothing; a strutting rooster, a he-goat, and a king with his army around him"
Proverbs 30:29-31, NIV

Proverbs 30:29-30

Stateliness, in the Christian life, is a spiritual dignity and composure which distinguishes the believer from the non-believer. The Bible is the handbook on this combination of virtues and our Lord the supreme Example. This numerical proverb helps us learn the fourfold secret of stateliness.

We must Show the Bravery of a Fighter

"There [is] that [which is] stately in [its] stride. . . . that [moves] with stately bearing: a lion, mighty among beasts, who retreats before nothing" (vv. 29-30, NIV). A lion never flees from his pursuers, whether they be men or beasts, but walks away at a slow and majestic pace. God intends that the believer should know this quality of bravery. That is why Solomon says, "The righteous are bold as a lion" (Prov. 28:1). To be bold as a lion means that we must fight the *world* (1 John 5:4), the *flesh* (1 Cor. 9:25-27), and the *devil* (James 4:7).

We must Show the Victory of a Winner

"There [is] that [which is] stately in [its] stride. . . . that [moves] with stately bearing: . . . . a strutting rooster" (vv. 29, 31). This conjures up the mental picture of the fighting cock and the prize winner. The general idea is plain. We are not only to be fighters, but winners. This is why the Bible has so much to say about rewards. Only those who win are eventually crowned with the crowns of incorruptibility (1 Cor. 9:25-27), righteousness (2 Tim. 4:8), rejoicing (1 Thess. 2:19), glory (1 Pet. 1:3-4), and life (James 1:12).

We must Show the Dignity of a Leader

"There [is] that [which is] stately in [its] stride. . . . that [moves] with stately bearing: . . . . a he-goat" (vv. 29, 31). The picture here is of a he-goat marching at the head of the herd with the dignity and strength of a leader. Significantly, leaders are referred to as he-goats in other parts of Scripture (Dan. 8:5, 21, NASB). Nothing inspires confidence like the dignity of a true leader. This is why we are to fix our eyes on Jesus (Heb. 12:2). Our Lord, in turn, expects us to be leaders of the flock of God (see 1 Pet. 5:2-4, 8-9, NIV). In our bearing and confidence we should be like the he-goat, expressing confidence in a willing, worthy, and watchful leadership.

We must Show the Mastery of a Ruler

"There [is] that [which is] stately in [its] stride. . . . that [moves] with stately bearing: . . . a king with his army around him" (vv. 29, 31). As Christians, we are to display the mastery of a ruler. Throughout Scripture believers are described as those who reign (see Rom. 5:17, NIV; 2 Tim. 2:12; Rev. 5:10). As kings, we should live and serve with stateliness and sovereignty, demonstrating the mastery of a rulership over all our words and deeds.

The word "stately," which occurs twice in our text and nowhere else, is an interesting one. It literally means "beautiful." Our English dictionary defines the word as "imposing dignity." In a culture eroding morally, ethically, and spiritually every day before our eyes, somebody with *stateliness* stands out! What was it that attracted little children, common people, and needy sinners to the Master's side? It was an attractive stateliness. Stateliness is not snobbishness, it is the sweetness of a Walter Payton!

O beautiful Savior, glorious Lord! When You brought creation into being You declared it was "very good." Can it be any different when You bring Your "New Creation" into redemptive visibility? I thank You that You can take up the broken pieces and "make something beautiful out of my life!" You even borrow from Your animal creation to demonstrate "stateliness." Lord, make me more like You. Amen.

Wifehood

*"Who can find a virtuous wife
[a noble wife]? For her worth
is far above rubies"*
Proverbs 31:10

Wifehood

"Who can find a virtuous wife [a noble wife]? For her worth is far above rubies"
Proverbs 31:10

Proverbs 31:10-31

The verses before us constitute one of the most glorious tributes to womanhood to be found in Holy Scripture. In this closing chapter Solomon shares the advice of a godly mother (v. 1) concerning the quality and dignity of a noble wife.

The Worth of a Noble Wife

"Who can find a virtuous wife? For her worth is far above rubies" (v. 10). What Solomon is saying is that a noble wife is of inestimable worth, and cannot be purchased with the price of the most precious jewels. In his description of her essential worth the preacher passes over the superficial attractions, which men consider so important, for the characteristics of favor and beauty that can never be found in any strange and seductive woman. So Solomon goes deeper than face and grace to the essential worth of a model wife. She is a woman who has *the fear* and *the favor* of the Lord (v. 30).

The Work of a Noble Wife

"Give her of the fruit of her hands. And let her own works praise her in the gates" (v. 31). There are few passages in the Word of God which so clearly set out the scope of the ministry of a married woman as this one. With rare skill and deep insight, Solomon delineates the work of a perfect wife in terms of *service to her husband* (vv. 11-12). A perfect wife's service to her husband is one of love and loyalty; consequently, her husband trusts her. Such is the uniting bond of love that they share. She also provides *service to her family* (vv. 28-29). The ministry of a mother must be such that her children and husband will rise up to pay her honor and homage. This calls for a Christ-honoring example, Bible-centered instruction, and Spirit-anointed discipline in the home. *In service to her household,* the three dominant characteristics are energy, efficiency, and economy (see vv. 13-19). In *service to her neighbors* (vv.

20-25), her attitude is one of friendliness and helpfulness, extending to the poor, and reaching out to the needy.

The Words of a Noble Wife

"She opens her mouth with wisdom, and on her tongue is the law of kindness" (v. 26). The final test of a noble woman is what happens when she opens her mouth. First, there is *the substance* of her conversational life. Nothing is more refreshing, inspiring, and edifying than to listen to a woman *who has something substantial to say*. Happy is the woman who satisfies her heart in Christ and His Word, with the church and its work, with nature and its wonders, with literature and enriching reading, with life and current affairs, with music and poetry, and not least, with her husband's vocation—its problems and potentials. Such a wife will never open her mouth without speaking wisdom. Secondly, there is *the spirit* of her conversational life. It matters not only what a person says, but how it is said. The law of kindness is nothing less than the law of love. No one can be so sweet, tender, and charming as a woman whose tongue is controlled by the law of love which, of course, presupposes the indwelling and infilling of the Holy Spirit (see Rom. 5:5). It is truly remarkable and commendable that thirty–one chapters should bring us to this closure! To be called to a life of marriage, family, and service in the Lord, as described in this last chapter, is a little bit of "heaven on earth"!

O God, You saw that it was not good for man to live alone and brought to his side a helper comparable to him. You have forever hallowed this union and declared that a man leave Father and Mother and be joined to his WIFE. In a day of broken homes and dysfunctional families, restore us to the duty, beauty, and glory we have considered in this final devotional. I pray this earnestly in Jesus' name. Amen.

Your Devotional Life

I consider our daily walk with God to be the most important discipline in our lives. Indeed, the devotional life is the barometer of our spiritual condition. We are no better in public life than what we are in private life with our God.

A survey conducted by *Christianity Today* revealed that the average person prays only *three* minutes a day![1] That is hard to believe, but the facts are there to convict us.

Another survey showed that 93% of students preparing for the ministry in a well-known theological college confessed that they had no devotional life.

With this in mind, I want you to turn with me to a verse in the Gospel of Mark, Chapter 1 and verse 35. We read: "In the morning, having risen a long while before daylight, He [Jesus] went out and departed to a solitary place; and there He prayed." Let us look at the setting and then the sequel to our text.

The Lord Jesus, portrayed by Mark as God's perfect Servant, had had a very busy day; in fact, His full day had been protracted into a full evening. He, therefore, needed a long night's rest! But this matchless Servant considered it necessary to rise a great while before day to depart into a solitary place for prayer.

---

[1] April 6, 1979, p. 52.

In the light of such an example, none of us can excuse our devotional life on the grounds of a busy program, and certainly none of us can afford to forego our daily Quiet Time with the truth of this verse before us. For while it is true that Christ is seen here in His manhood as the perfect Pattern, we must remember that He was the God-man; and if He needed a regular prayer time, how much more you and me.

Then observe the sequel. When Peter and the others had sought Him out, even to His quiet place of prayer, their first words were, "Everyone is looking for You" (v. 37). The obvious lesson in these significant words is that prayer and a life of spiritual power go together; they are inseparably joined by God.

With these preliminary considerations, let us now examine our text more closely. The Greek reads: "Very early, while yet night, having risen up, He went out and departed into a desert place, and there was praying." If you would develop your devotional life:

You Must Have a Period for Prayer in Your Daily Program

"And *very early*, while yet night, having risen up, He went out and departed into a desert place."

When I speak about a period for prayer in the daily program, I am not overlooking the fact that prayer is both an attitude and an activity of the soul. There is a sense in which you and I should be living in the atmosphere of prayer moment by moment throughout the day. This is clearly implied in such statements as, "Men always ought to pray and not lose heart" (Luke 18:1); and again, "Pray without ceasing" (1 Thess. 5:17). You and I can be praying while we are driving the car, or jogging down the street, or digging in the garden. But having said that, it must be part of our devotional discipline to have a period for prayer in our daily program. From our text we learn that:

The Period for Prayer Must Have Priority

"*And very early*, while yet night, having risen up, he . . . prayed."

Ward Beecher once said, "Let the day have a blessed baptism by giving your first waking thoughts to God. The first hour of the morning is the rudder of the day."

John Trapp reminds us that "the most Orient pearls are generated out of the morning dew."

Jesus said, "Seek first the kingdom of God and His righteousness, and all these things shall be added to you" (Matt. 6:33).

If we would pray well we must pray early. Christ knew the value of the morning hours, so He made this period for prayer a matter of priority.

The Period for Prayer Must Have Prearrangement

"*While yet night*, having risen up." This was prearranged.

The quiet hour never comes fortuitously. In fact, the time for prayer never comes without prearrangement; the devil sees to that. The Word of God exhorts us to do "all things . . . decently and in order" (1 Cor. 14:40).

All great men of God have been those who have prearranged to give God the first hours of their day. We read that Abraham rose up early in the morning to worship (Gen. 22:3), Jacob rose up early in the morning to make his vows (Gen. 28:18), Joshua rose up early in the morning to sanctify himself (Josh. 3:1), Gideon rose up early in the morning to seek God's answer (Judg. 6:38), Samuel rose up early in the morning to ask for guidance (1 Sam. 9:26), David rose up early in the morning to battle for God (1 Sam. 17:20), and our text, of course, gives us the supreme example.

Dr. Vance Havner used to say: "Every Christian should determine a time and place for his devotions that work best in his own case. Our Lord [rose up a great while] before day and went to a solitary place to pray. I live on the road most of the time and the place changes but I rise early. I do so, not because Ben Franklin said it makes one healthy, wealthy and wise for it has not necessarily done that in my case! Early rising may be just a sign of old age, and some get up early just to brag about it. But still I believe we ought to start the day early and honor God with our first thoughts while the mind is clear and the day is still unspoiled.

"One great spiritual giant [claimed] that he could not get through the day without several hours of prayer. Yet another, just as great, said he could not pray long prayers. There is no uniform pattern. Let a man pray and read his Bible in the way that best meets his needs. Early hours pay off in the benefit of quietness before the rat race begins . . . Americans in general and preachers in particular have lost the art of meditation. It is a rare sight to behold any man just walking and thinking, like Isaac in the fields at eventide. I pray better walking than kneeling, and better early than late. The man who begins his day without meeting God is taking a frightful risk of spiritual defeat in the hours ahead. In man's last days when we face the stepped-up opposition of the powers of darkness as never before, what fools we are if we do not gird on [the armor of God]."[2]

The Period for Prayer Must Have Purposefulness

"Having risen up, He prayed."

This reveals the deliberate purposefulness of Jesus. The word "prayed," as G. Campbell Morgan observes, is more than asking. It suggests the going forward of desire, not only for God's gifts, but for Himself. You will find the purpose of this early period for prayer in Isaiah 50, verses 4-5: "The Lord God has given Me the tongue of the learned, that I should know how to speak a word in season to him who is weary. He awakens Me morning by morning, he awakens My ear to hear as the learned. The Lord God has opened My ear; and I was not rebellious, nor did I turn away." I want you to notice, in passing, three things about our Lord's daily devotional life:

There was Devotional Openness. "Morning by morning, He awakens [or opens] My ear." Our Lord never—and I mean never—missed his Quiet Time. Every morning He was open to the voice of His Father. Like Samuel, His daily request was, "Speak, Lord, for Your Servant hears" (1 Sam. 3:9).

George Mueller discovered this secret and wrote: "I saw that the most important thing I had to do was to give myself to the reading of the Word of God and to meditation on it [in order that I] might be comforted, encouraged,

[2] "The Breakfast of Champions" *Pulpit Helps*, published by AMG Publishers, Chattanooga, TN 37422.

warned, reproved [and] instructed. . . . I began . . . to meditate on the New Testament . . . early in the morning. The first thing I did, after having asked in a few words the Lord's blessing upon His precious Word, was to begin to meditate on the [Scriptures], searching as it were into every verse to get blessing out of it; not *for the sake of the public ministry of the Word, not for the sake of preaching on what I had meditated upon, but for the sake of obtaining food for My own soul.*"[3] George Mueller called this "Soul Nourishment First"; and you and I can never receive such nourishment without this openness to the Lord day by day. I might add that if the Word does not open to us then it is because there is sin in our lives. God is more willing to speak to us than we are to listen. But if we have grieved or quenched the Spirit then we must seek cleansing and forgiveness in order to hear that still, small voice.

There was Devotional Obedience. "He [opened] My ear to hear as the learned. The Lord God has opened My ear; and I was not rebellious, nor did I turn away."

Your spiritual life is determined by one supreme word in the Christian vocabulary, and that is *obedience*. There is no substitute for obedience. "To obey is better than sacrifice, and to heed than the fat of rams" (1 Sam. 15:22). All the sacrifice of your ministry, your preaching, your giving, even the laying down of your life, means nothing if it isn't backed by total obedience to God's Word.

The apostle John employs several illuminating expressions to show aspects of obedience: e.g., *dwelling in Christ* means that we obey what He

[3] George Mueller, *Soul Nourishment First* (Bristol: The Mueller Homes for Children), p. 1.

says—"He who keeps His commandments abides in Him" (1 John 3:24). *Abiding in the light* means "He who loves his brother abides in the light" (1 John 2:10). *To know God* requires obedience to His will—"By this we know that we know Him, if we keep His commandments" (1 John 2:3). *To love God* is also equivalent to obedience—"By this we know that we love the children of God, when we love God and keep His commandments" (1 John 5:2). So we see that all fellowship with God is based upon obedience. The question is, is your obedience up-to-date?

There was Devotional Overflow. "The Lord God has given Me the tongue of the learned, that I should know how to speak a word in season to him who is weary."

The natural overflow of a devotional life is the ability to speak a word in season to needy men and women around us. The Bible reminds us that "out of the abundance of the heart the mouth speaks" (Matt. 12:34). The reason why our lives are often so stale is because we haven't spent time alone with God. It does not take long to detect whether or not a fellow Christian is walking with God. What overflows is obviously what is occupying his heart and mind. Sit down with a bunch of people and hear them talk and you will soon know whether or not they have been in the presence of Jesus. Of the early apostles it was said, "They realized that they had been with Jesus" (Acts 4:13).

"The shining face of Moses did not come from a hurried call at heaven's gate; it was obtained by dwelling in the Lord's presence for forty days. The skill of David in slinging stones wasn't obtained when he met Goliath; it was by practice in the wilderness. The blessing of Pentecost came after tarrying in prayer. If we would know the Spirit's [power] we must [wait] in His presence."[4]

You Must Have a Place for Prayer in Your Daily Program

"He went out, and departed into a solitary place, and there prayed." The Lord Jesus had no conveniences for securing quiet and privacy—but He made them. The hilltop was His closet, the sod His praying mat, and the darkness His bolted door.

These words, "a solitary place," teach a principle which our Lord emphasized elsewhere: "When you pray, you shall not be like the hypocrites. For they love to pray standing in the synagogues and on the corners of the streets, that they may be seen by men. Assuredly, I say to you, they have their reward. But you, when you pray, go into your room, and when you have shut your door, pray to your Father who is in the secret place; and your Father who sees in secret will reward you openly" (Matt. 6:5-6). The reason why our Lord emphasizes the closed door and secrecy is because:

Prayer Must Have Solitude

"He departed into a solitary place, and there prayed."

There is a vast difference between private and corporate prayer. Each type of prayer brings blessing after its kind, but there is a difference. Corporate prayer is less exacting. There is a sense of fellowship that gives encouragement and inspires expression, but such prayer has a tendency to do

[4] F. E. Marsh

its thinking by proxy. In private prayer the soul stands naked and alone in the presence of God. Thought is personal, prayer is original, and motive is challenged. Who can measure the influence of such an hour spent alone with God?

J. Wilbur Chapman tells how he met the famous missionary, Praying Hyde. Chapman asked the man if he would come to his room and pray for him personally. He was conducting meetings at the time, and felt he needed to be strengthened by the Holy Spirit. Hyde was very obliging and consented to his request. Chapman says that as soon as they were in his room, the missionary locked the door and dropped to his knees. "I waited 5 minutes without that dear man uttering a single syllable," said Chapman. "Presently I felt hot tears course down my cheeks. Although Hyde had said nothing, I knew I was in the presence of God in a special way. Then with upturned face and eyes streaming, he exclaimed, 'O God!' Then he was quiet again. When he sensed that he was in full communion with the Lord, there came from the depths of his heart petitions such as I had never heard. I [rose] from my knees knowing what real prayer was."[5] Prayer like this requires solitude.

Prayer Must Have Silence

"A solitary place." Samuel Chadwick says that the soul needs its "silent spaces." Prayer should not be merely talking to God, but rather listening to Him through the ears of the soul. God's purpose and plan for our lives can only be known through the silent waiting on Him in the light of His Word and the illumination of the Holy Spirit.

---

[5] Henry G. Bosch in *Our Daily Bread* (Grand Rapids: Radio Bible Class), March 28, 1979.

I want to confess and tell you that the greatest moments of my Quiet Time are not when I am pouring out my heart in adoration—wonderful as that is—or pouring out my heart in confession, or pouring out my heart in petition, or pouring out my heart in intercession. The greatest moments of my Quiet Time are when I wait silently and say, "Speak, Lord, Your servant hears" (1 Sam. 3:10), and I allow the Holy Spirit to lift from the Word of God such truths as He would teach me in that hour. Prayer needs its "silent spaces."

Prayer Must Have Sincerity

"A solitary place." Only when we are shut up with God can we truly be sincere. This is why hypocrites can never pray in secret. Prayers that are a pretense require an audience; but in the solitary place of prayer hearts have to be pure and hands clean, or they dare not close the door and be alone with God who sees us in secret. Insincerity can never live in the shadowless presence of God. It would revolutionize the lives of most Christians if they were shut in with God in some solitary place of prayer for an hour each day. No one can really be shut in with God until he has first withdrawn himself from things; yes, and from people, and this is much harder. Even among Christians he who withdraws himself from society to pray is sometimes considered as "too zealous." Not only is it true that the world is too much with us, we are too much with men, and not enough with God. No wonder we have weak Christians, weak churches and weak defenses against sin. We have not yet withdrawn enough from men to prevail over men. Prevailing with men is a secret learned only in the prayer room with God.

I was talking to a pastor about his private life and asked, "Brother, how did you ever get into such a mess? Do you have a daily Quiet Time? Do you shut yourself away in your study? Do you close that door and insist, 'Do not disturb'"? After a moment he replied, "If I did that I would go mad." I knew what he meant; he was scared.

Even when you kneel with your dear wife, who is closer to you than anyone else, you can be a hypocrite! Because you are praying in her presence you want to show her how spiritual you are; but when you are shut alone with God hypocrisy dies, hypocrisy withers, in the awesome presence of God. You have to be real.

One last thought I must share with you:

You Must Have a Pattern for Prayer in Your Daily Program

"And there [He] prayed."

Christ's pattern was not to say prayers, but to *pray*. Of Elijah it was said that he "prayed in his prayer" (James 5:17). Some of us need to ask ourselves, in the words of the children's hymn: "I often say my prayers, but do I really pray?"

No doubt it was because of occasions like this that the disciples requested, "Lord, teach us to pray" (Luke 11:1). The fact is that they never chanced upon our Master in prayer without finding Him *really* praying. You will remember that the Lord gave the answer to their question in what we know as *the pattern prayer*: "Our Father in heaven, hallowed be Your name. Your kingdom come. Your will be done on earth as it is in heaven. Give us this day our daily bread. And forgive us our debts, as we forgive our debtors. And do not lead us into temptation, but deliver us from the evil one. For Yours is the kingdom and the power and the glory forever. Amen." (Matt. 6:9-13).

Among other things that I could say I want to stress three aspects as well as attitudes of a life of prayer.

Prayer Should Reflect the Devotion of a Son

"Our Father in heaven, hallowed be Your name."

What is greater, what is sweeter, what is purer, than the enjoyment of filial fellowship and love in the presence of your father? Will you turn to John, Chapter 17? We call this the High Priestly Prayer. In twenty-six short verses the Lord Jesus refers six times to God as His Father. Verse 1: "Father"; verse 5: "O Father"; verse 11: "Holy Father"; verse 21: "Father"; verse 24: "Father"; verse 25: "O righteous Father." Notice the progression: "Father"; "O Father"; "Holy Father"; "O righteous Father"—*the devotion of a Son*. And there is no earthly son who doesn't know the exquisite, inexpressible joy of talking with his father—reveling in his presence, hearing his voice, telling his father how much he loves him.

Prayer Should Reflect the Submission of a Servant

"Your kingdom come. Your will be done."

The learning of God's will, and the adjustment of my will thereto is a very important part of prayer. God's *kingdom* and *will* are central in the whole prayer. That's where we say with Saul of Tarsus, "Lord, what do You want me to do?" (Acts 9:6).

When this aspect of prayer is understood, there is no such thing as the problem of unanswered prayer. You see, *direct* answers, *delayed* answers, or *denied* answers, are all answers when the life is submitted to the will of God. *This is where the Word of God comes into play.*

In my booklet, *Manna in the Morning*,[6] I outline what I do in my own Quiet Time, in relation to the Word of God. I read the Bible quite differently from how I read it in family prayers or study periods. With the passage open before me, I read it generally, then I read it specially. Finally, I read it personally and I ask myself the following questions: "What is God saying to me? Is there some promise that I am to claim? Is there some example I am to follow? Is there some sin I am to avoid? Is there some command I should obey? Is there some new thought about God the Father, God the Son, God the Holy Spirit? Some new thought about the devil? What is today's thought? What is God saying to me? And I never leave the passage until I am prepared to write down what God has said to me in order that I may pray back to Him those very things which He has said to me. I believe that was a secret of Paul's great prayers that you find throughout his Epistles. They are full of Scripture, and they were just the outgoing of his heart, having met with God in the light of the Word. And as you pray back to God what God has already said to you, your will is adjusted to His will, so that now you can go out into His kingdom world to establish on earth what God has already said in heaven.

---

[6]Stephen F. Olford, *Manna in the Morning*, available from Olford Ministries International, P. O. Box 757800, Memphis, Tenn. 38175-7800.

Prayer Should Reflect the Petition of a Suppliant

"Give us this day our daily bread. And forgive us our debts, as we forgive our debtors. And do not lead us into temptation, but deliver us from the evil one."

First, there is *the daily business*. "Give us this day our daily bread." William Barclay informs us that some time ago "a papyrus fragment turned up with this word 'daily' on it; and the papyrus fragment was actually a woman's shopping list! Against an item on her list was this word 'daily.' It was a note to remind her to buy supplies of a certain food for the coming day. So, very simply, what this petition means is 'give me the things we need to eat for the coming day.'"[7]

As believers, we have a hundred and one matters that concern our daily needs. Nothing is insignificant or unimportant in the sight of God. He who marks the fall of a sparrow and numbers the very hairs of our head is interested in the details of our home, our church, and our life generally. As suppliants, we must come to God in simple faith, believing that He will hear our requests and answer our prayers.

Secondly, there is *the daily burden*. "Forgive us our debts, as we forgive our debtors." Our Lord never had to pray these words because He was "holy, harmless, undefiled, [and] separate from sinners" (Heb. 7:26). At the same time, He carried the burden of human sin upon His heart and eventually bore that burden on Calvary's cross in order that we might know forgiveness and cleansing.

---

[7]William Barclay, *The Gospel of Matthew*, vol. 1, rev. ed. (Philadelphia: The Westminster Press, 1975), p. 217.

But you know, as well as I do, that the burden of sin is a constant issue in our walk with God. Sometimes we commit private sin, and we have to confess it alone with God. Other times we commit personal sins, and we have to go and put it right with our brother, for Jesus said, "If you bring your gift to the altar, and there remember that your brother has something against you, leave your gift there before the altar, and go your way. First be reconciled to your brother, and then come and offer your gift" (Matt. 5:23-24). Sometimes it is public sin, when we have to share our burden with the whole church. The point is that if we do not put it right with others we cannot expect God to forgive us. In fact, He has made our willingness to forgive others the basis for the experience of divine forgiveness in our own personal lives. Jesus said: "If you forgive men their trespasses, your heavenly Father will also forgive you. But if you do not forgive men their trespasses, neither will your Father forgive your trespasses" (Matt. 6:14-15). Let us see to it that we "walk in the light as he is in the light," and only then shall we know perfect cleansing of the precious blood (1 John 1:7).

Thirdly, there is *the daily battle*. "And do not lead us into temptation, but deliver us from the evil one." There is nothing wrong with temptation. Even our Lord was tempted in the wilderness and elsewhere, but by the power of the Word and of the Spirit He was more than conqueror.

We, likewise, will be tempted by the devil every day of our lives, and particularly in relation to our devotional life. But you and I can know victory in Jesus. This is what John means when he says, "I have written to you, young men, because you are strong, and the word of God abides in you, and you have overcome the wicked one" (1 John 2:14). We are living in a demonic world. I believe that Satan is on his last rampage before the Lord Jesus comes back again. But thank God we can be overcomers, for the Bible reminds us that "He who is in [us] is greater than he who is in the world"; and again: "This is the victory that has overcome the world—our faith" (1 John 4:4; 5:4). As we trust the Lord Jesus to do in us and through us what we cannot achieve of ourselves we can be "more than conquerors through Him who loved us" (Rom. 8:37). Without this victory in our personal lives there can be no victory in our public lives. Your privilege, and mine, is to claim the victory for each day in the place of prayer, and then to go out to celebrate that victory in every area of life and ministry.

So we have seen what is meant by the devotional life, and I trust that what has been expounded will not only be instructional, but also inspirational. Nothing will substitute for the daily Quiet Time. The example of our Lord Jesus Christ not only demonstrates this, but demands similar action from you and me. We read, "In the morning, having risen a long while before daylight, He [Jesus] went out and departed to a solitary place; and there He prayed." Remember, the measure of your spiritual stature is not how you stand in your public life, but how you kneel in your private life!

> *This is the path the Master trod;*
> *Should not the servant tread it still?*

STEPS TO PEACE WITH GOD

1. **RECOGNIZE GOD'S PLAN—PEACE AND LIFE**

   The message you have read in this book stresses that God loves you and wants you to experience His peace and life.

   The BIBLE says . . . *"For God loved the world so much that He gave His only Son, so that everyone who believes in Him may not die but have eternal life." John 3:16*

2. **REALIZE OUR PROBLEM—SEPARATION**

   People choose to disobey God and go their own way. This results in separation from God.

   The BIBLE says . . . *"Everyone has sinned and is far away from God's saving presence." Romans 3:23*

3. **RESPOND TO GOD'S REMEDY—CROSS OF CHRIST**

   God sent His Son to bridge the gap. Christ did this by paying the penalty of our sins when He died on the cross and rose from the grave.

   The BIBLE says . . . *"But God has shown us how much He loves us—it was while we were still sinners that Christ died for us!" Romans 5:8*

4. **RECEIVE GOD'S SON—LORD AND SAVIOR**

   You cross the bridge into God's family when you ask Christ to come into your life.

   The BIBLE says . . . *"Some, however, did receive Him and believed in Him; so He gave them the right to become God's children." John 1:12*

THE INVITATION IS TO:

REPENT (turn from your sins) and by faith RECEIVE Jesus Christ into your heart and life and follow Him in obedience as your Lord and Savior.

PRAYER OF COMMITMENT

"Lord Jesus, I know I am a sinner. I believe You died for my sins. Right now, I turn from my sins and open the door of my heart and life. I receive You as my personal Lord and Savior. Thank You for saving me now. Amen."

If you want further help in the decision you have made, write to:
Billy Graham Evangelistic Association, P.O. Box 779, Minneapolis, MN 55440-0779

If you are committing your life to Christ, please let us know! We would like to send you Bible study materials and a complimentary six-month subscription to *Decision* magazine to help you grow in your faith.

The Billy Graham Evangelistic Association exists to support the evangelistic ministry and calling of Billy Graham to take the message of Christ to all we can by every prudent means available to us.

Our desire is to introduce as many as we can to the person of Jesus Christ, so that they might experience His love and forgiveness.

Your prayers are the most important way to support us in this ministry. We are grateful for the dedicated prayer support we receive. We are also grateful for those that support us with contributions.

Giving can be a rewarding experience for you and for us at the Billy Graham Evangelistic Association (BGEA). Your gift gives you the satisfaction of supporting an organization that is actively involved in evangelism. Also, it is encouraging to us because part of our ministry is devoted to helping people like you discover and enjoy the stewardship of giving wisely and effectively.

Billy Graham Evangelistic Association
P.O. Box 779
Minneapolis, Minnesota 55440-0779
www.billygraham.org

Billy Graham Evangelistic Association of Canada
P.O. Box 841, Stn Main
Winnipeg, Manitoba R3C 2R3
www.billygraham.ca

Toll free: 1-877-247-2426